ARAB-AMERICAN RELATIONS IN THE PERSIAN GULF

D0871664

ARAB-AMERICAN RELATIONS
IN THE PERSIAN GULF

Emile A. Nakhleh

American Enterprise Institute for Public Policy Research
Washington, D. C.

Emile A. Nakhleh is associate professor of political science at Mount Saint Mary's College, Emmitsburg, Maryland.

ISBN 0-8447-3154-4

Foreign Affairs Study No. 17

Library of Congress Catalog Card No. 75-4005

Printed in the United States of America

CONTENTS

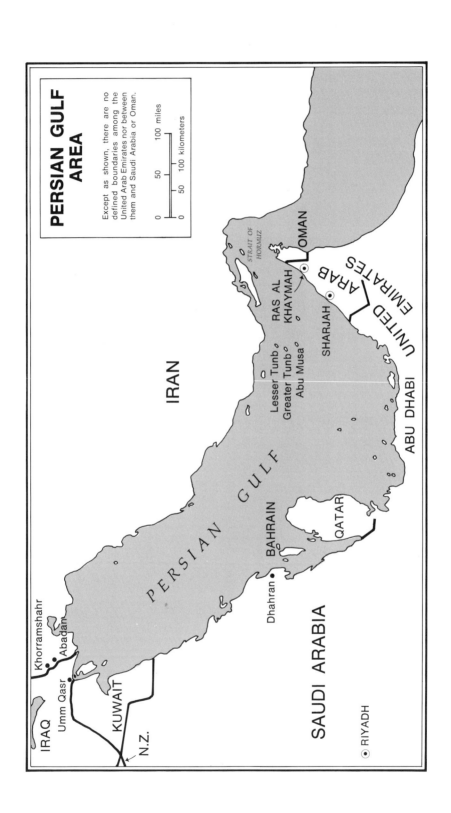

PERSIAN GULF
AREA

Except as shown, there are no
defined boundaries among the
United Arab Emirates nor between
them and Saudi Arabia or Oman.

0   50   100 miles
0   50   100 kilometers

IRAQ
Khorramshahr
Umm Qasr
Abadan
KUWAIT
N.Z.

IRAN

PERSIAN GULF

Dhahran

BAHRAIN

QATAR

SAUDI ARABIA

RIYADH

Lesser Tunb
Greater Tunb
Abu Musa

RAS AL
KHAYMAH

SHARJAH

STRAIT OF
HORMUZ

OMAN

UNITED ARAB
EMIRATES

ABU DHABI

INTRODUCTION

The Arab/Persian Gulf[1] has assumed important economic and strategic dimensions in recent years. Because of their immense oil reserves, the gulf littoral states have truly become the world's economic center of gravity, and because of the gulf's proximity to the Soviet Union and to the Indian Ocean, the region also has a strategic significance which cannot be ignored by the United States. Limited by market demand and by the necessity of persuading the diverse oil-producing states to present a united front, this newly discovered oil power is a somewhat delicate mechanism for influencing international politics. The October 1973 War,[2] however, demonstrated that under the proper conditions oil sanctions can be a potent short-term weapon.

Before the October War, the gulf Arab states regarded oil primarily as an economic asset with little connection to the larger political order, either regionally or internationally. This position was frequently reiterated by no less than the giant oil-producing country of Saudi Arabia. The United States, as the world's largest consumer of oil and as a country with traditionally friendly relations with Saudi Arabia, had accepted the Saudi separation of oil and politics as a major premise of its Middle Eastern policies. Therefore, the Saudi decision during the October War to combine oil and politics and to relate the flow of Saudi oil to American Middle Eastern policies

---

[1] The Arab/Persian Gulf, hereinafter referred to as the gulf, comprises the following countries: Iran, Iraq, Kuwait, Saudi Arabia, Bahrain, Qatar, the United Arab Emirates (Abu Dhabi, Dubai, Sharja, 'Ajman, Umm al-Qaywayn, Ra's al-Khayma, Fujayra) and the Sultanate of Oman.

[2] Cultural/religious biases are apparent in the names which the Arabs and Israelis have given to this war. The Arabs refer to it as the Ramadan War; the Israelis, the Yom Kippur War. The author feels that the October War is a sufficiently neutral term.

1

marked a major deviation from a long-standing policy. The Saudi stand was firmly endorsed by all Arab oil-producing countries, both individually and as members of the Organization of Arab Petroleum Exporting Countries (OAPEC). This unexpected turn of events has forced a major re-thinking of American interests and long-range policies by American decision makers toward all Arab national interests, particularly the specific regional interests of the gulf.

Beyond the element of surprise, which recent reactions in American Mid-East policy have realistically minimized, the entanglement of oil and politics has forced American policy makers to recognize three realities. First, it is naive to talk of international economics as isolated from international politics. Arab oil production can no longer be treated separately from Arab national issues, most particularly the Palestine problem. Second, smoothly functioning economic relationships (the United States learned painfully during the October War) will follow only if outstanding political conflicts are resolved. Again, the Palestine conflict is the uppermost issue. Third, the United States, as a major industrial country and as a superpower directly concerned with international peace and security, can no longer choose between one of only two traditional positions: complete detachment or total involvement. Other options must be examined.

In political and economic conflicts, solution by proxy (from the United States viewpoint), that is, to stand back and let local powers solve their problems by themselves, has been proven a faulty option during and since the October War.[3] American policy need not be aggressive, and indeed it often is not. But commensurate with its superpower status, the United States's economic and strategic interests transcend the country's borders—a fact which the United States must always recognize and for which it must make no apologies. Recent successful efforts to bring about a partial solution of the Arab-Israeli conflict are indicative of the United States's newly emerging posture in its Middle Eastern international relations: an active concern for resolution of the conflict and a broadly defined but effective commitment to the advancement of peace. It is against this background that American long-range interests in and relations with the Arab/Persian Gulf can be understood, and it is in this context that the United States must devise a long-range policy perspective within which a new relationship will emerge between this country and the countries of the gulf.

---

[3] For a thorough examination of new policy considerations, see Congressional Quarterly, *The Middle East: U.S. Policy, Israel, Oil and the Arabs* (Washington, D. C.: Congressional Quarterly, Inc., 1974), pp. 3-7.

Since this study concerns itself with Arab-American relations in the gulf, U.S.-Iranian relations, another cornerstone of the American presence in the region, fall outside the scope of this study. It must be emphasized, however, that the United States's relations with Iran can be viewed only as a part of the total American posture in the gulf. Simultaneously, Iran's role in the gulf cannot be considered in isolation, nor has this role been designed to function in a vacuum.[4]

In order to develop a policy framework for future American relations with the Arab littoral states of the gulf, several dimensions will be examined. The following sections of this study will examine the political and ideological nature of the Arab regimes in the gulf, the religious/tribal foundations of these regimes and the oil-generated affluence of their ruling families, the diplomatic and military activities of regional and other powers, and the new economic factor in the gulf. The last chapter of this study will then present a long-range projection of American international relations in the gulf and the spectrum of options available to U.S. policy makers.

---

[4] For an examination of Iran's role in the Gulf, see Rouhallah K. Ramazani, *The Persian Gulf: Iran's Role* (Charlottesville, Virginia: University Press of Virginia, 1972).

1
THE POLITICAL/
IDEOLOGICAL DIMENSION

An Overview

Although differences exist in the internal dynamics of each state on
the Arab littoral coast of the Persian Gulf, all states share one over-
whelming characteristic in the eyes of the world: collectively they
exercise a considerable influence on the world's economy through
their oil. The United States may be less dependent on Arab oil than
Western Europe or Japan, but it is fast becoming a major consumer
and is therefore more concerned with the societies of the gulf region.

The similarities of these countries are evident in their political
and social cultures, as well as in their geography and demography.
Before proceeding into the political culture of gulf societies, let us
briefly examine the physical environment, geography and population,
in which this tribally based political culture has developed.[1]

Other than Bahrain, an archipelago located in the middle of the
gulf approximately fifteen miles from the Arab coast and one hundred
and fifty miles from the Iranian coast, the Arab states are all situated
on the eastern periphery of the Arabian Peninsula. They all share
two common boundaries: the gulf to the east and Saudi Arabia to the
west. Saudi Arabia itself spreads across the Arabian Peninsula from
east to west, thereby giving it an opening on the gulf and a long

---

[1] Among several contemporary studies on this aspect of the gulf are: Donald
Hawley, *The Trucial States* (New York: Twayne Publishers, Inc., 1971); *Area
Handbook for the Peripheral States of the Arabian Peninsula* (Washington, D. C.:
U.S. Government Printing Office, 1971); James Belgrave, *Welcome to Bahrain*
(Manama, Bahrain: The Augustan Press, 1973); *Qatar into the Seventies* (Doha,
Qatar: Ministry of Information, 1973); Bernard Gérard, *Qatar* (Doha, Qatar:
Ministry of Information, 1974); *Dawlat al-'Imarat al-'Arabiyya al-Muttahida*
[The United Arab Emirates] (Abu Dhabi: Center of Research and Archives, 1972).

coast on the Red Sea. The Sultanate of Oman borders on the Indian Ocean.

Except for the agricultural basins in Iraq in the north and Oman in the south, all gulf Arab states basically endure a hot, arid climate with a meager annual rainfall that rarely exceeds three inches. Humidity is high along the coast. Vast regions of these countries are desert where Arab tribes and their camel herds have roamed for centuries. There are four topographic formations: (a) the mountainous zone in Oman and Ra's al-Khayma; (b) the gravel plains to the west of the mountains; (c) a coastal strip of marshes, sandy limestones, salt flats and shales; and (d) the sand country, which consists of sand dunes and gravel.[2] In addition to oil, it is believed that certain minerals, such as nickel and copper, might also be found in the Arabian Peninsula.[3] Available estimates of the total area under consideration in this study run to between 900,000 and 1,000,000 square miles.[4] In the narrow green strip of fertile land, agriculture traditionally has been limited to cultivating date palms and some few vegetables. Almost without exception, gulf Arab states import all of their foodstuffs, including flour, dairy products and meat. Coastal areas historically have relied on fish for the mainstay of their diet.

The population of the Arab gulf, which available estimates put at approximately 7 million,[5] is primarily Muslim Arab. The first striking demographic characteristic of most of these countries is the presence of large expatriate minorities among the population, mostly in the labor class. Excluding Saudi Arabia and Oman, for which detailed population data are not available, the estimated percentages of the expatriate populations run from as high as 60 percent in Qatar to approximately 20 percent in Bahrain. In Kuwait, Abu Dhabi, and Dubai expatriates constitute over 50 percent of the total population.[6] Most of the expatriate labor is located in the lower and higher levels of the employment spectrum, for example, household staff and skilled

---

[2] Hawley, *The Trucial States*, pp. 281-284.

[3] For an excellent geological study of the region see *Geology of the Arabian Peninsula: Sedimentary Geology of Saudi Arabia* (Washington, D. C.: U.S. Government Printing Office, 1966).

[4] Bahrain, 250 square miles; Kuwait, 6,000; Oman, 82,000; Qatar, 5,000; Saudi Arabia, 830,000; and the United Arab Emirates, 32,000. *World Data Handbook* (Washington, D. C.: U.S. Department of State, 1972), p. 8.

[5] Bahrain, 216,000 people; Kuwait, 700,000; Oman, 600,000; Qatar, 130,000; Saudi Arabia, 5,500,000; and the United Arab Emirates, 200,000. Ibid. (with modifications). This discussion primarily pertains to the lower gulf, thereby excluding Iraq.

[6] These estimates are based on population statistics from 1970 onward.

workers. Due to stringent citizenship laws, expatriates have a very low expectation of becoming naturalized citizens of these countries.[7]

A significant characteristic of the native populations is the relatively high percentage of young people, primarily school-age children; it must be remembered, too, that functional literacy rarely exceeds 50 percent. Also, most of the population is located in metropolitan areas. In fact, several amirates are basically no more than city-states.[8] Although several thousand Bahrainis live in villages outside the two metropolitan centers of Manama and Muharraq, the very small size of the country effectively discourages any development of a rural population.

Politically, each of the Arab countries of the gulf is ruled by one who is selected, usually on a basis of primogeniture, from the ruling family in that state. With varying degrees, the type of rule in most of these states is autocracy based on tribal tradition and family rule. The political systems of these states are treated in the following section of this chapter.

Political Infrastructures and Dynamics

Much has been written about the gulf from a geo-strategic and economic point of view, but there is a paucity of literature dealing with the internal political dynamics of the region. Little information is available for English language readers on the processes of institutional modernization presently afoot in the individual countries of the region. Although the present political regimes in the region are basically similar, three official descriptions are used for the states involved: Saudi Arabia is referred to as a kingdom, Oman, as a sultanate, and Kuwait, Bahrain, Qatar and the United Arab Emirates are known as amirates or sheikhdoms. Iraq officially designates itself as a republic. Besides Saudi Arabia, which is the oldest independent state in the region (1932), all other states of the lower gulf have become independent since 1970, the year of Oman's independence. Bahrain, Qatar and the United Arab Emirates all became independent in 1971. Kuwait became independent in 1961.

---

[7] The four largest groups of expatriates are Iranians, Indians, Pakistanis (primarily in Bahrain, Dubai, Abu Dhabi and Qatar) and Palestinians (in Kuwait, Qatar and Abu Dhabi).

[8] As an example, the populations of at least three amirates of the United Arab Emirates do not exceed 10,000 each. Moreover, in each of the seven amirates which constitute the United Arab Emirates, the capital, from which the amirate derives its name, is the only major town in the country.

Before independence the gulf amirates were British protectorates, linked to Great Britain by special agreements, which were concluded early in the nineteenth century, ostensibly to combat piracy. Following Britain's decision in 1968 to terminate its special treaties with gulf amirates and to withdraw its military presence from the gulf by the end of 1971, the nine amirates [9] directly affected by the British decision began serious attempts to form some sort of federation that would come into being immediately following British withdrawal. Eventually only seven united to form the United Arab Emirates, with Bahrain and Qatar choosing separate paths.

Several factors contributed to the failure of the nine amirates' efforts in the period 1968–1971 to unite into a federation. The proposed federal structure was a hurried reaction to the announced British withdrawal, and the call for federation was prompted by leaders of the individual amirates determined to preserve their rule. Secondly, several border disputes were still outstanding, the most important of which was the one between Saudi Arabia and Abu Dhabi over the Buraimi Oasis. Third, the relations between the different ruling families were charged with traditional jealousies and suspicions. The disparities in wealth, education and population among the amirates added fuel to the fire. Fourth, Iran's long-standing territorial claim to Bahrain, which was resolved peacefully in 1970–1971, kept Bahrain from pushing for a federation which Iran at that time opposed. The agreement signed in Dubai on 27 February 1968 that announced the birth of the Federation of Arab Amirates was never executed, and the federation collapsed two and a half years later.[10]

Following the collapse of the federation and encouraged by the resolution of Iran's territorial claims, Bahrain declared itself independent on 14 August 1971. Qatar followed suit on 1 September and the remaining amirates united to form the United Arab Emirates on 2 December 1971.[11] The three new states became full members of both the League of Arab States and the United Nations during the first year of their independence.

---

[9] Bahrain, Qatar, Abu Dhabi, Dubai, Sharja, 'Ajman, Umm al-Qaywayn, Ra's al-Khayma and Fujayra. For background information on this question, see John Duke Anthony, "The Union of Arab Amirates," *The Middle East Journal* (Summer 1972), pp. 271-287.

[10] For a thorough treatment of the story of this federation see Riyad Nagib al-Rayyis, *Sira' al-Wahat wa al-Naft: Humum al-Khalij al-'Arabi Bayna 1968-1971* [Struggle of Oases and Oil: Troubles of the Arabian Gulf, 1968-1971] (Beirut, Lebanon: al-Nahar Press, 1973).

[11] The United Arab Emirates was initially composed of six amirates: Ra's al-Khayma joined the United Arab Emirates on 10 February 1972.

No discussion of the internal dynamics of these countries would be complete without some mention of the tribal backgrounds of the ruling families. The ruling families of the gulf Arab countries (twelve in all) derive from tribes which came out of the central and northern deserts of Arabia prior to and since the rise of Islam. In the eighteenth century they began to settle in the towns, islands and peninsulas which they presently rule. For example, the al-Khalifas of Bahrain and the al-Sabahs of Kuwait both belong to the Bani 'Utub clan of the 'Aniza tribal federation. The al-Sa'uds of Saudi Arabia also descend from al-'Aniza.[12] The Qawasim of Ra's al-Khayma and Sharja proudly trace their origins to the family of the Prophet Muhammad. Table 1 shows the different ruling families in each of the amirates and the names of present rulers. In every amirate the ruling family constitutes the wealthiest and most influential elite in the country.

With the advent of independence the Arab states emphasized building modern political and social infrastructures. Although relative progress has been achieved, authority has remained strongly vested in the person of the ruler and his family. In other words, the move toward constitutional monarchy has not eliminated the tribal source of legitimacy.

Although each one of the constitutions promulgated in Kuwait, Qatar, Bahrain, and the United Arab Emirates makes it clear that the state is democratic, popular elections have been held in only two: Kuwait and Bahrain. It should be remembered that rule is hereditary and the ruler's accession to power is not a matter of popular decision. Usually the inner councils of the ruling family decide who the heir apparent should be and ultimately who should rule. Members of the ruling family in each state occupy the most important cabinet posts and other high government positions. Table 2 provides an illustration of this point. In this ruling process the family is assisted by a small, indigenous elite of senior bureaucrats and influential businessmen. In most gulf societies, the influential families who are not members of the ruling family are usually prosperous merchants, since commerce has long been a traditional occupation in the gulf.

Concurrent with this tribal approach to government, the last decade has witnessed the advent of constitutionalism. Gulf states are presently in the midst of transforming from one-man autocratic tribal rule to a more or less popular form of government. Although the new constitutions describe the new governmental processes as being demo-

---

[12] Ahmad Abu Hakima, *Early History of Eastern Arabia: The Rise and Development of Bahrain and Kuwait* (Beirut, Lebanon: Khayats, 1963).

Table 1

RULING FAMILIES IN THE ARAB/PERSIAN GULF (1974)

Amirate/State	Ruling Family	Tribe	Ruler	Date of Accession
Bahrain	al-Khalifa	Bani 'Utub	Shaikh 'Isa bin Sulman al-Khalifa	1961
Kuwait	al-Sabah	Bani 'Utub	Sh. Sabah al-Salim al-Sabah	1966
Oman	al-Taymur	al-Bu Sa'idi	Sultan Qabus bin Sa'id al-Taymur	1970
Qatar	al-Thani	Tamim-Bani 'Utub	Sh. Khalifa bin Hamad al-Thani	1972
Saudi Arabia	al-Sa'ud	al-Sa'ud	King Faysal bin 'Abd al-'Aziz al-Sa'ud	1966
United Arab Emirates			Sh. Zayid bin Sultan al-Nhayyan	1971
Abu Dhabi	al-Nhayyan	Bani Yas (al-Bu Falah)	Sh. Zayid bin Sultan al-Nhayyan	1966
Dubai	al-Maktum	Bani Yas (al-Bu Falasah)	Sh. Rashid bin Sa'id al-Muktum	1958
Sharja	al-Qasimi	al-Qawasim	Sh. Sultan bin Muhammad al-Qasimi	1972
'Ajman	al-Na'imi	al-Na'im (al-Bu Khurayban)	Sh. Rashid bin Humayd al-Na'imi	1928

Umm al-Qaywayn	al-Mu'alla	al-'Ali	Sh. Ahmad bin Rashid al-Mu'alla	1929
Ra's al-Khayma	al-Qasimi	al-Qawasim	Sh. Saqr bin Muhammad al-Qasimi	1948
Fujayra	al-Sharqi	al-Sharqi	Sh. Muhammad bin Hamad al-Sharqi	1952*

* Died 17 September 1974.
Source: Author's survey.

Table 2

MINISTERIAL POSTS: BAHRAIN AND QATAR (1974)

Ministry	Bahrain	Qatar
Ruler	Sh. 'Isa bin Sulman al-Khalifa	Sh. Khalifa bin Hamad al-Thani
Prime Minister	Sh. Khalifa bin Sulman al-Khalifa [a]	Sh. Khalifa bin Hamad al-Thani [c]
Defense	Sh. Hamad bin 'Isa al-Khalifa [b]	Sh. Hamad bin Khalifa al-Thani [b]
Foreign Affairs	Sh. Muhammad bin Mubarak al-Khalifa	Sh. Suhaym bin Hamad al-Thani [a]
Interior	Sh. Muhammad bin Khalifa bin Hamad al-Khalifa	Sh. Khalid bin Hamad al-Thani [a]
Education	Sh. 'Abd al-'Aziz bin Muhammad al-Khalifa	Sh. Jasim bin Hamad al-Thani [a]
Municipalities	Sh. 'Abdalla bin Khalid al-Khalifa	Sh. Muhammad bin Jabr al-Thani
Justice	Sh. 'Isa bin Muhammad al-Khalifa	Sh. 'Abd al-Rahman bin Sa'ud al-Thani
Finance and National Economy	Mr. Mahmud Ahmad al-'Alawi	Sh. 'Abd al-'Aziz bin Khalifa al-Thani [b]
Development & Engineering Services	Mr. Yusif Ahmad al-Shirawi	[d]
Labor & Social Affairs	Mr. Ibrahim Muhammad Hmaydan	Mr. 'Ali bin Ahmad al-Ansari

Ministry		
Cabinet Affairs	Mr. Jawad Salim al-'Urayyid	
Legal Affairs	Dr. Husayn Muhammad al-Baharna	
Health	Dr. 'Ali Fakhru	
Information	Mr. Tariq 'Abd al-Rahman al-Mu'ayyid	
Economy and Commerce		Mr. Khalid Muhammad al-Mani'
Electricity and Water		Mr. 'Isa Ghanim al-Khawari
Public Works		Sh. Nasir bin Khalid al-Thani
Communications & Transportation		Sh. Jasim bin Muhammad al-Thani
Industry & Agriculture		Mr. Khalid bin 'Abdalla al-'Atiyya
		Mr. 'Abdalla bin Nasir al-Suwaydi
		Sh. Faysal bin Thani al-Thani

a Ruler's brother.

b Ruler's son.

c The ruler also holds the title of Prime Minister (no heir apparent has yet been named in Qatar).

d Blank space indicates this cabinet post nonexistent.

Source: Author's survey.

cratic, one must be careful not to compare this peculiarly gulf venture into democracy to any specific democratic form of government in the West. The process of transformation from classical tribalism into an urban and affluent form of tribalism is a very delicate one, employing a gradual and evolutionary method of political reform.

The constitutions that have been promulgated in Kuwait (12 November 1962), the United Arab Emirates (18 July 1971), Qatar (2 April 1970, amended 22 April 1972) and Bahrain (6 December 1972) have several common principles:

(1) Family rule is to continue in these states on a hereditary basis.

(2) These states are a part of the Arab world and their peoples constitute a part of the Arab nation.

(3) Islam is the official religion of the state and Arabic is the official language.

(4) Islamic law is a primary source of legislation.

(5) At least theoretically, government is divided into three branches: the executive headed by the Amir (ruler); the legislative, headed by a nationally elected body; and the judiciary.[13]

(6) Welfare statism is the primary guideline in the state's relationship to its citizens.

Of the four constitutions, only those of Kuwait and Bahrain have become fully operational; the Qatari and the United Arab Emirates constitutions are still referred to as provisional.[14] The Bahraini constitutional experiment closely parallels that of Kuwait in principles and general national development.[15]

Although Kuwait was the first amirate to promulgate a constitution, the Bahraini and Qatari experiments in modern government are more directly relevant to future constitutional development in the lower gulf. Certain points in the Bahraini and Qatari constitutions are indicative of the direction that political transformation might take in these societies. Specific indicators of this process are: how the sources of legitimacy are defined, to what degree popular participation is permitted and how authority is shared among the divisions of government.

---

[13] Only in Kuwait and Bahrain has a national assembly actually been popularly elected. In Qatar and the United Arab Emirates such a body is called *majlis al-shura* (Advisory Council), and it has so far been an appointed body.

[14] In the United Arab Emirates, the member amirates still retain their autonomy and independent internal governmental structures. The provisional constitution is primarily a federal document.

[15] In fact, Kuwait's constitutional expert on short-term loan to Bahrain, helped write Bahrain's draft constitution and the first election law.

14

On legitimacy, the Bahraini constitution establishes several fundamental principles. First, "Bahrain is a sovereign independent Islamic Arab state,"[16] and second, "Bahrain's rule is hereditary, vested in the person and descendants of Shaikh 'Isa bin Sulman al-Khalifa, from father to his eldest son."[17] Third, "the system of government in Bahrain is democratic, and the people are the source of authority,"[18] and fourth, "Islam is the official religion of the state, and Islamic law (shari'a) is *a* primary source of legislation."[19] Fifth, "the Amir is the head of state, and his person is protected and above reproach."[20] The Qatari constitution establishes similar sources of legitimacy. First, "Qatar is a sovereign independent Arab state,"[21] and second, "Islam is the official religion and Islamic law is *the* primary source of legislation."[22] Third, "the system is democratic,"[23] and fourth, "the Amir is the head of state, and his person is protected and above reproach."[24] Fifth, "the rule in the state is hereditary, vested in the family of al-Thani."[25]

On the question of popular participation, the Bahraini constitution makes several explicit statements. First, as was pointed out above, the people are considered the source of authority,[26] and members of the National Assembly are popularly elected by secret ballot according to law.[27] The freedoms of conscience, speech, press, correspondence and organization are protected by law,[28] and "members of the National Assembly represent the whole people."[29] The Qatari constitution refers to popular participation in government, but only obliquely. The people's role in government is discussed only in future

---

[16] *Constitution of the State of Bahrain, al-Jarida al-Rasmiyya* [The Official Gazette] (6 December 1973), Article 1, Section A. (Hereafter referred to as the *Constitution of Bahrain.*)

[17] Ibid., Section B.

[18] Ibid., Section D.

[19] Ibid., Article 2. (Emphasis added.)

[20] Ibid., Article 33.

[21] *The Provisional Amended Basic Law of Government in the State of Qatar, al-Jarida al-Rasmiyya* [The Official Gazette] (22 April 1972, Article 1). (Hereafter referred to as the *Constitution of Qatar.*)

[22] Ibid. Note the difference in the two countries' positions on Islamic law and legislation. (Emphasis added.)

[23] Ibid.

[24] Ibid., Article 20.

[25] Ibid., Article 21.

[26] See footnote 17.

[27] *Constitution of Bahrain*, Article 43, Section A.

[28] Ibid., Articles 22, 23, 24, 26 and 27.

[29] Ibid., Article 63, Section A.

terms, to be realized once the "transitional stage,"[30] presently served by the provisional constitution, comes to an end. At this stage even the Advisory Council (a semi-parliament) is appointed by the ruler and participates only indirectly in legislation. Council members usually represent the prominent families in the community.[31] Once the transitional stage comes to an end, which will be decided later by an amiri decree, and once a permanent constitution is promulgated, the Advisory Council would be popularly elected by secret ballot.[32]

Although both constitutions call for the division of government into three branches, the Bahraini constitution is again more explicit on the sharing and distribution of authority among the branches. The system of government is based on the separation of powers among the legislative, executive and judicial branches.[33] Unlike the separation of powers in Western democracies, however, the legislative branch in Bahrain is headed jointly by the ruler and the National Assembly; the ruler also heads the executive branch, and judicial decisions are always rendered in his name.[34] Legislative bills become law once they pass the National Assembly and are ratified by the ruler.[35] The judiciary is independent and autonomous,[36] and judges should not be subjected to undue influence from any source.[37]

The Qatari constitution also divides the government into branches, but only two are named separately and explicitly: the executive, headed by the ruler in cooperation with the Council of Ministers,[38] and the judiciary, in which court decisions are rendered in the name of the ruler.[39] The only reference to the legislative branch under this section of the constitution is that the ruler promulgates laws upon the suggestion of the Council of Ministers and after consulting the Advisory Council.[40]

The above political indicators reveal several points:

(1) As an evolutionary process of reform, political development in the gulf seems to be a synthesis of traditional tribalism and modern democracy.

---

[30] *Constitution of Qatar.* Preamble.
[31] Ibid., Articles 40-43.
[32] Ibid., Article 46.
[33] *Constitution of Bahrain*, Article 32, Section A.
[34] Ibid., Section B.
[35] Ibid., Article 42.
[36] Ibid., Article 101, Section A.
[37] Ibid., Section B.
[38] *Constitution of Qatar*, Article 18.
[39] Ibid., Article 19.
[40] Ibid., Article 17.

16

(2) Although modern government in the gulf relies on secularist principles, the body politic is solidly based on Islam.

(3) The Bahraini political system seems to be at a more advanced stage than the Qatari system in terms of popular participation in government, government accountability and popular sovereignty.

The Qataris' adherence to Islamic law reflects the traditionalism which is prevalent in the lower gulf. The relative political liberalism in Bahrain's constitution, which is largely due to the higher levels of education and political sophistication in Bahrain, remains futuristic as far as other gulf societies are concerned, and religious conservatism is still a strong and influential force in the region. Yet it is also apparent that political development is the wave of the future in the gulf and that this wave will definitely be affected by strongly conservative socio-religious residues in these new political formations.

Ideological Support of Politics

The discussion of ideology in this section is limited to one basic perspective: the impact of ideology on political stability in the gulf. This study assumes that ideology and stability are directly related to present and future political and economic ties among the states themselves and between these states and the outside world. Political developments within the last five years have proven the correctness of this assumption, especially from the point of regional security and America's strategic posture in the region. The United States is obviously concerned with the ideological aspect of political development, for American long-range interests in the gulf will be greatly enhanced or harmed by the type of ideological doctrines that will emerge and by the power and influence of the ideological movements espousing these doctrines. Although the interaction of ideology and diplomacy will be treated in the following chapter, particularly in regard to the United States's policy options in the region, it would be useful at this juncture to discuss the interaction between ideology and the nature and direction of the whole process of political development and transformation in the new gulf. In this regard, such concepts as political traditionalism, dissent, reform and revolution acquire new significance, and the rise of radical movements become of paramount importance.

While under British protection, the common ideology that swept the Arab gulf in the fifties and sixties could be summed up in one word: nationalism. Save for rare exceptions, Arab nationalism was vocally expressed by only a few elites, mostly labor leaders; it was directed against the British presence and against those local leaders who cooperated with and benefited from the status quo. Invariably, in every amirate the ruling family was a beneficiary of the British presence.

The best organized and most effective nationalist movement in the fifties was in Bahrain. This was primarily because a labor tradition had existed for some time in Bahrain (oil production in Bahrain began in 1932) and because the educational system in the country—the first in the gulf—dated from 1919. Several Bahraini leaders became prominent in the nationalist movement, both in the gulf and throughout the Arab world.[41] Other nationalists appeared in Muscat and Oman during that period, but nowhere else in the lower gulf. The nationalist movement in Iraq in the north has a long-established history and has had a completely different development than that of the lower gulf; as such it falls outside the scope of this study.[42]

In spite of the rise of nationalism in the fifties and sixties, political stability and internal security were maintained under the imperial umbrella of *Pax Britannica*. Fears for future political stability in the gulf began to be voiced in Western circles following the 1968 announcement by the British government that it would withdraw its military presence from east of Suez. By the end of 1971, however, all British-protected amirates (sheikhdoms) had emerged as independent states.

In building their political societies, leaders of the new states began to face new challenges and demands for political reform. The transformation of these societies into modern, viable political entities has centered around one main question: if political development is to be an evolutionary process, at what rate of change should this process proceed in order to transform the society, yet avoid revolution? In other words, could traditional tribalism gradually change into a functional political system without being destroyed by its own contradictions? Is the tribal system of rule, which is simply based on a one-man government supported by a ruling family, capable of transforming itself from within into a modern system of government which can accommodate unprecedented popular demands for a more open government? Can the tribal/Islamic principle of *shura*, the basis of

---

[41] For a thorough analysis of the nationalist movement in Bahrain in the fifties see 'Abd al-Rahman al-Bakir, *Min al-Bahrain ila al-Manfa* [From Bahrain to Exile] (Beirut, Lebanon: Dar Maktabat al-Haya, 1965).

[42] For an excellent analysis of political developments in Iraq in this century see two works by Majid Khadduri, *Independent Iraq, 1932-1958* (New York: Oxford University Press, 1961) and *Republican Iraq: A Study of Iraqi Politics Since the Revolution of 1958* (New York: Oxford University Press, 1969).

family rule in the sheikhdoms for centuries, reconcile itself to the introduction of new partners into the decision-making process on the government level without totally undermining the heretofore unquestioned authority of the ruler?

The present rulers of the Arab gulf states have answered all of these questions in the affirmative. The al-Sabahs of Kuwait, for example, point with pride to their country's constitutional development and parliamentary participation in government over the last decade. They also point to the presence of an active press with ideological leanings from extreme right to extreme left. The al-Sabahs are also proud of the complex economic and social infrastructures which have been constructed in the Kuwaiti state. The al-Sabahs exhibit these accomplishments as an indication that the new political system is working, which in turn implies that the process of transformation from a tribal autocratic rule into a modern governmental system has been successfully accomplished.

The al-Khalifas of Bahrain, as a second example, point to similar, albeit more recent, political successes since independence. Such things as the election of a Constitutional Assembly in 1972 (the first such popular election in Bahrain's history), the new constitution, the election of a National Assembly in 1973 are to them tangible indications of the successful transformation into modern government. In a recent statement to the press, the prime minister of Bahrain referred to the free parliamentary debates in the country as unarguable proof that democracy is truly at work in Bahrain.[43]

Shaikh Khalifa bin Hamad al-Thani, the ruler of Qatar, has also pointed to recent political development in the country as an indication that political transformation can be successfully accomplished under his rule. He emphasized that the "opening up" of the regime on the political level must be guarded and gradual. The ruler promised that this process would ultimately lead to the building of a better society in whose government the citizens of Qatar would participate actively and positively.[44] The provisional constitution, the creation of the Advisory Council and the establishment of a modern public administration are indicators of the successful adaptation of desert tribal rule to a modern urban setting. Similar positions in support of a tribal/modern government synthesis have been taken, although in varying degrees, by Shaikh Zayid bin Sultan al-Nhayyan of the United Arab Emirates (Abu Dhabi) and Sultan Qabus bin Sa'id bin Taymur of Oman.

---

[43] *al-Adwa'* (Bahrain), 8 August 1974.
[44] *al-'Arab* (Qatar), 24 June 1974.

The major change-oriented ideology, which has rejected any possibility of marrying serious political reform to a tribal system of government, is represented in the Popular Front for the Liberation of Oman and the Arabian Gulf (PFLO). The PFLO, which has recently dropped "and the Arabian Gulf" from its title,[45] has been supported by the People's Democratic Republic of Yemen (South Yemen) and to a lesser degree by China and the Soviet Union. The Popular Front for the Liberation of Oman, as it is now called, is the moving force behind the Dhufar rebellion against the regime of Sultan Qabus in Oman. In recent years, PFLO has operated through local branches throughout the amirates of the lower gulf (previously the Trucial Coast) and Bahrain, but has confined its organized military activities to Oman. In Oman itself, the Sultan has relied heavily on British military help and, since December 1973, on Iranian troops and advisors [46] in his campaign against Dhufari rebellion.[47]

The radicalism of the PFLO stems from its rejection of the family-supported status quo and from its commitment to a total systemic change in these regimes to bring about widespread popular participation in government. The PFLO believes that the democratization process of internal politics means by definition the end of tribalism and the elimination of family rule. Although the impact of this ideology will be discussed more fully in the following chapter, suffice it to say at this point that the popular front's ideology has been unanimously viewed as the arch-enemy of stability and orderly government by every gulf regime, including those of Iran and Saudi Arabia. The United States has officially accepted this view as well, and gulf governments have mustered all their resources to combat the threat to internal stability which they see in the PFLO.[48]

Because of its labor tradition and educated elites, Bahrain has been a somewhat fertile ground for change-oriented ideologies (nationalism, Ba'thism, socialism, and revolutionism), such as the doc-

---

[45] *Sada al-'Usbu'* (Bahrain), 13 August 1974.

[46] For an account of the landing of Iranian paratroopers in Oman see a special report entitled "Details of the Iranian Invasion" in the leftist weekly *al-Tali'a* (Kuwait), 12 January 1974, pp. 15-18.

[47] For additional reading on this question see 'Adil Rida, *'Uman wa al-Khalij: Qadaya wa Munaqashat* [Oman and the Gulf: Issues and Debates] (Cairo, Egypt: Dar al-Kitab al-'Arabi, 1969); Zakariyya Nil, *Bu'rat al-Khatar fi al-Khalij al-'Arabi* [Center of Danger in the Arabian Gulf] (Cairo, Egypt: al-Ahram Publishing House, 1974); and *The Arabian Peninsula, Iran and the Gulf States: New Wealth, New Power, A Summary Record* (Washington, D. C.: The Middle East Institute, 1973).

[48] Internal security departments throughout the gulf states have often exchanged intelligence on the clandestine activities of PFLO or PFLO-suspected activities in the region.

trine espoused by the PFLO. During the campaigns of the 1972 and 1973 national elections to the Constitutional Assembly and the National Assembly, the popular front determinedly tried to discourage the electorate from participating in the election. Despite the PFLO efforts, approximately 88 percent of all registered voters voted in each election. The political demands of the PFLO centered on the following major points: (1) To allow the basic individual freedoms of opinion, press and assembly; (2) to grant labor the right to unionize; and (3) to release all political prisoners and to allow political exiles to return to their respective countries.[49] Since the PFLO believed at the time (1972) that popular elections in Bahrain were nothing more than an attempt at face-saving, it called on the people not to cooperate. The PFLO failed in its endeavor, however, and Bahraini elites welcomed the opportunity to participate in the constitutional experiment.

The PFLO has more recently been accused of fomenting trouble against family regimes, particularly among the workers. The 1974 labor strikes in Bahrain and the ensuing confrontation between labor leaders and the government is a typical example. The Bahraini government officially accused certain outside, "irresponsible" elements of creating internal dissension to undermine the democratic experiment in the country.[50] The government was supported in this claim by several nationalist reform-oriented members of the National Assembly and by Bahrain's leading newspapers.[51]

Although the PFLO principally advocates political reform, it also endorses economic socialism and supports certain Marxist-Leninist doctrines on the state and the individual. To such religiously conservative family regimes as these, the popular front's doctrines are anathema and a potential source of political disorder and violence. This attitude has prompted these leaders to tacitly support Iranian military operations in Oman against the popular front in Dhufar on behalf of the sultan.[52]

There is no doubt that the future course of political development in the gulf will be closely linked to the predominant ideology. The need for political reform is evident to elites of all ideologies. They

---

[49] From a PFLO statement issued in August 1972.

[50] For selected newspaper reports on the labor-government confrontation in Bahrain during 1974 see *Gulf Weekly Mirror* (Bahrain), 16 June 1974; *al-Siyasa* (Kuwait), 17 June 1974; *Sada al-'Usbu'* (Bahrain), 25 June 1974; *al-Adwa'* (Bahrain), 20 June 1974; and *al-Adwa'*, 8 August 1974.

[51] See a poignant editorial on this subject entitled "Lest the Seeds of Communism Hatch Here," in *al-Adwa'*, 20 June 1974.

[52] *al-Tali'a* (Kuwait), 12 January 1974, p. 3.

differ mainly in the method to be used to bring about such reform, and the method itself will determine to a large extent the responsiveness of the government in power and ultimately the orderliness of the transformation process.

Goals and Options: The Arab Gulf States

Every state selects from a set of policy options a certain final course of action designed to realize one or more of the goals which the state has set for itself. In this section, we will examine the goals and policy options of the Arab gulf states as they relate to internal political development. How these states view political change within their own societies, what path such change should take and how they propose to bring about the desired change will be discussed. The following section will then deal with the United States's goals and options vis-à-vis domestic political development and change in these societies. Although several theoretical studies [53] have been written on the science of decision making and several case studies have been published,[54] the examination of goals and options in this study is designed to deal with a specific region and a specific set of given facts.

The selection of any one policy alternative in regard to an issue, a conflict or a set of problems by any one state in the gulf or by the United States is an integral part of that state's entire decision-making process. For purposes of analysis, Elmer Plischke [55] has established three layers of goals: the national purpose, the basic goals and the foreign policy system.[56] He described the national purpose as being "the overriding, all pervading, motivating drive of a people, which is identifiable to and identified by the body politic, and which imbues the government and people with a willingness to endure sacrifice for its achievement." [57] The basic goals, which constitute the second layer in the Plischke model, may be defined as those goals which, if

[53] For example, see Harold Lasswell, *The Decision Process: Seven Categories of Functional Analysis* (College Park, Maryland: University of Maryland, 1965); Charles E. Lindbom, *The Policy-Making Process* (Englewood Cliffs, New Jersey: Prentice-Hall, 1968).

[54] For example, see Theodore Sorensen, *Decision-Making in the White House* (New York: Columbia University Press, 1963); Robert F. Kennedy, *Thirteen Days: A Memoir of the Cuban Missile Crisis* (New York: W. W. Norton & Company, Inc., 1971).

[55] For a very useful and succinct discussion of options and policy making, see Elmer Plischke, *Foreign Relations Decisionmaking: Options Analysis* (Beirut, Lebanon: Catholic Press, 1973).

[56] Ibid., p. 16.

[57] Ibid.

achieved, would ensure national identity and national security, preserve the peace and promote general welfare.[58] The third layer of goals is concerned with the pursuance of immediate policy objectives.[59]

In an advanced political system such as the American one, decision making is a complex process that takes many variables into consideration. Former Secretary of State Dean Rusk is quoted to have observed that in making decisions a State Department officer "takes his bearings from the great guidelines of policy, well-established precedents, the commitments of the United States under international charters and treaties, basic statutes, and well-understood notions of the American people about how we are to conduct ourselves." [60] The complexity of establishing one's national goals often reflects the stage of development of the state's political system. Being new states with embryonic political systems in which decision making is relatively simple and unidimensional, the process of selecting national goals on the domestic level is still uncomplicated for the Arab gulf states.

To gulf governments, the overriding goal in regard to domestic politics is the establishment of relatively open political systems in which the ruling family in each state would more or less share its authority to rule with a carefully nurtured citizenry, and in which political order, stability and harmony would prevail. Islam, Arab traditions and gulf tribal customs would constitute the ideological cornerstones of the envisioned system. Both Shaikh Khalifa bin Hamad al-Thani, the ruler of Qatar, and Shaikh Khalifa bin Sulman al-Khalifa, prime minister of Bahrain, have recently expressed these very goals in separate press interviews.[61]

Using the simple query option analysis,[62] it is possible to delineate the options available to gulf leaders to realize their national goal. Of the several available alternatives, the two extremes would not be plausible options: (a) to ruthlessly crush all opposition and dissent to the ruling family's conception of the new society; or (b) to allow individual freedoms to flourish unchecked, hoping that a free society would finally establish its own societal equilibrium. In spite of their inclination toward continued family rule, gulf rulers realize that total suppression of their people would ,ot necessarily produce an orderly society. On the other hand, several gulf rulers

---

[58] Ibid., p. 17.

[59] Ibid.

[60] Ibid., pp. 7-8.

[61] al-'Arab (Qatar), 24 June 1974 and al-Bahrain al-Yom [Bahrain Today], 8 August 1974.

[62] Plischke, Foreign Relations Decisionmaking, p. 20.

have stated that their peoples are not yet ready, socially and educationally, for the heady atmosphere of political freedoms (organizations, parties, unions, et cetera). In between these extremes other options present themselves.

The main option concerned with the building of a domestic political structure that gulf governments have chosen since independence has encompassed the following policies:

(1) Establish and expand a system of free public education. College and university students are being encouraged in their academic pursuits and financially supported by government. Political activities among college students, however, are systematically discouraged.

(2) A guarded venture into popular participation has been attempted. The political stratum has been invited to work within the recently established parliamentary system; at the same time popular political behavior has been closely monitored by intelligence agencies. Secret political activity has not been tolerated at all and serious opposition has been systematically and selectively removed.

(3) In almost every new gulf political state a constitution has been promulgated which, while recognizing the existence of limited individual freedoms, has given the ruler tremendous powers as head of the state. Such a constitution effectively insures the continuation of family rule. No labor unions have been allowed to exist and no political parties have been organized.

Gradualism and controlled political development have been the cornerstones of the policies of these new states. Once the political appetites of the elites have been whetted, however, can gradualism continue to function? How can the process be safely speeded up? Gulf rulers hope that, in time, their approach will prove successful.

Goals and Options: The United States

In recent years American officials have stated on several occasions their perception of security and stability in the gulf, a view that will be developed more fully in the next chapter. Parallel to this regional view, American goals concerning domestic political stability within the individual countries can be summarized in one main point: to help maintain domestic stability, as symbolized by the "shaikhly" status quo. This goal has been overshadowed by the American regional overview, and as a consequence no clear American policy options have been worked out concerning gulf domestic political development.

By various economic, political, military and cultural agreements with the governments of these states, the United States government indirectly has expressed confidence in the current status quo. In addition, the United States has viewed with favor the efforts of Sultan Qabus to liquidate the rebellion in Dhufar and the active military assistance which the shah of Iran has rendered to the sultan of Oman in this endeavor. The United States has officially referred to the PFLO, which spearheads the Dhufari rebellion, as a movement of terrorists and destructive elements. The CENTO conference, which was held in Teheran in April 1973, indirectly encouraged Iran to play a more active role in regional security. The landing of Iranian troops in Oman, ostensibly at the request of Sultan Qabus, in December 1973 was a direct expression of the American view of domestic security.[63]

Aside from this policy, the United States has not taken any active policy posture toward domestic political reform. Neither has the United States shown any appreciable interest in domestic political developments in the individual states. The surprised reaction of American decision makers toward the results of the 1973 national elections in Bahrain, in particular the victory of eight leftist candidates, revealed that the United States assessment of Bahraini politics was outdated. Fortunately the 1974 decision of the American government to raise the level of American diplomatic representation throughout the lower gulf to the level of full ambassadors is a correct option, long overdue.

A desirable option would seem to be active support of gradual but perceptible political reform. These governments could be helped to realize that pluralism based on divergent political views within a political system is a natural result of the expanded popular base of government. Since the United States goal of political stability complements that of local regimes, it would seem possible to formulate some form of long-range cooperation that would transcend the individual regimes and enhance the prospects for political evolution.

---

[63] *al-Tali'a*, 12 January 1974.

2
THE DIPLOMATIC/
MILITARY DIMENSION

An Overview

The gulf's economic and strategic importance to the United States cannot be overemphasized. In public forums, congressional hearings and press conferences, American officials have constantly referred to the United States's direct and expanding interests in the region.[1] Although the United States has signed several military and commercial agreements with gulf powers, the future of American relations and influence in the region today hangs in a precarious balance and demands a serious, ongoing reassessment of policies. The fact that American general goals in the region can be easily delineated does not mean that the policy options available to American decision makers are as easily implemented.

It is generally agreed that American goals in the gulf include support of regional security arrangements, advocacy of peaceful settlement of territorial disputes, continued accessibility to oil supplies and the enhancement of American economic interests.[2] But what makes the realization of these goals difficult is the heterogeneity of interests, ideologies, cultures and states in the region. Aside from

---

[1] The following congressional hearings illustrate this interest: U.S. Congress, House, Committee on Foreign Affairs, *U.S. Interests in and Policy Toward the Persian Gulf*, 92d Congress, 2d session (Washington, D. C.: U.S. Government Printing Office, 1972); *New Perspectives on the Persian Gulf*, 93d Congress, 1st session (Washington, D. C.: U.S. Government Printing Office, 1973); *Oil Negotiations, OPEC, and the Stability of Supply*, 93d Congress, 1st session (Washington, D. C.: U.S. Government Printing Office, 1973); and *Proposed Expansion of U.S. Military Facilities in the Indian Ocean*, 93d Congress, 2d session (Washington, D. C.: U.S. Government Printing Office, 1974).

[2] A statement by Joseph Sisco, assistant secretary of state for Near Eastern and South Asian Affairs, before the Subcommittee on the Near East and South Asia, House Committee on Foreign Affairs, *New Perspectives on the Persian Gulf*, p. 2.

Iran, the Arab gulf states, though they exhibit certain cultural political and economic similarities, represent different, often opposing ideological trends and interests; and because of the disparities in capability (wealth, population, territory), the influence exerted by these states regionally and internationally is of varying degree. The role that each state expects to play in regional politics would be a function of at least three factors: (1) the state's own concept of regional collective security and consequently its desire to participate in any regional security arrangements, (2) the state's ideological leanings, particularly concerning internal political reform and development and the state's willingness to coexist with neighboring states with opposing ideologies, and (3) the state's actual capability to choose those policy options concomitant with the influence it expects to exert regionally.

For example, republican, Ba'thist-controlled Iraq has a definite view of collective security that has been often described as revolutionary. It is diametrically opposed to any form of Iranian hegemony in the gulf. Iraq also favors extensive internal political reform in its neighboring countries, and Iraq-American relations have been correct at best and icy at worst. Both Iran and Saudi Arabia have had warm relations with the United States despite the Saudi oil embargo following the October War, yet they differ on the substance and method of regional security. Bahrain is the only gulf state to have signed a military agreement with the United States, or any major power, which has resulted in the stationing of American naval personnel on its soil. The military rebellion in Oman is another variable that must be contended with. Several gulf governments perceive a real threat to their existence from the radical ideology espoused by this rebellion.

This ideological/cultural mosaic notwithstanding, most gulf states and amirates share several common characteristics:

(1) They all are oil producers, collectively owning the world's largest reservoir of known oil reserves.

(2) The majority of the population is Muslim Arab with a common cultural heritage. Iran's population is Muslim of the Shi'ite sect, but not Arab.

(3) Most gulf states are ideologically conservative, and the regimes are basically autocratic.

(4) Although gulf states have in recent years embarked on a new path of industrialization, their economies are still technically developing.

(5) Since the educational tradition is relatively recent, these states would for the foreseeable future remain in definite need of outside experts and technical and scientific assistance.

(6) Although they are financially capable of purchasing whatever military equipment they require, gulf states are still dependent on foreign powers for their security.

(7) Most gulf states are involved in yet unresolved boundary and other territorial disputes, which means that the potential for future conflict in the region is still present.

(8) Although they are sovereign independent states, although they have their own goals and objectives, although in oil they possess a formidable weapon and although they will soon amass among themselves the world's largest hard currency reserves, the gulf states remain subject to the policies of the superpowers. The strategic importance of the gulf by necessity draws superpower politics into gulf affairs, and these states must react to this involvement.

In this chapter an attempt shall be made to assess the regional and international politics of the region, the military posture of the gulf states, their concept of collective security, and finally the United States posture in terms of goals and objectives in the region.[3] Diplomacy in the gulf and the interaction of goals and policies of regional and foreign powers are part of a complex process which operates on several levels. The gulf is part of a larger sphere of international activity in which these powers act upon each other and are in turn acted upon to produce a balance of interests. Both the gulf states and the United States are vitally concerned with the smooth functioning of this balancing process. The gulf is an extension of the Indian Ocean, and it is the eastern frontier of the Arab world. It is the lifeline of European, Japanese and American industry, and it borders on the Soviet Union. Gulf states, save Iran, formally do not belong to defense alliances, yet the region constitutes a link between CENTO/SEATO in Asia, NATO in Europe and the Warsaw Pact in Eastern Europe. Locally, gulf governments staunchly oppose the radicalism of movements like the PFLO, yet they strongly support the Palestine revolution on the other side of the peninsula.

In order to further examine the supports of this complex equilibrium, let us consider the relationship of these various interests as an interaction of two spheres: the Arab presence and the Iranian

---

[3] For a succinct presentation of the gulf's importance in international politics, see Enver M. Koury, *Oil and Geopolitics in the Persian Gulf Area: A Center of Power* (Beirut, Lebanon: The Catholic Press, 1973).

presence. The interaction of interests and policies between these two spheres focuses on regional cooperation, regional radicalism, Iranian hegemony and general regional diplomacy.

Regional Diplomacy: The Arab Presence

The Arab presence in the gulf may be divided into two groups of states. The conservative or moderate group encompasses Kuwait, Bahrain, Qatar, the United Arab Emirates, Oman and Saudi Arabia; the latter is the center of conservatism in the region. The second group, which includes the People's Democratic Republic of Yemen and Iraq, may be best described as progressive, leftist, reformist and radical or revolutionary. The PFLO and the Dhufari rebellion obviously belong to the gulf's Arab left.[4]

The six states of the first group, which represent the Arab right, have several characteristics in common: tribal background, family rule, conservative political ideology, friendship with Western powers, including the United States, oil-generated wealth, and, of course, the Muslim religion. At the same time, several boundary disputes between these states still remain unsettled. Among them are the Saudi-Abu Dhabi-Omani boundary at the Buraimi Oasis,[5] the Abu Dhabi-Dubai boundary, the Saudi-Kuwaiti boundary and the Qatari-Bahraini boundary at the Hawar Islands. Other traditional jealousies between some of these states still exist. During the three years preceding independence (1968-1971), the nine amirates of the lower gulf attempted to unify themselves into one state. But, as we discussed earlier, the federation failed to materialize, and available information indicates that most, if not all, of the stumbling blocks in the path of federation were essentially procedural, not substantive. The points of contention included: (1) preparation of a provisional federal constitution, (2) selection of the federal capital, (3) the method of election/selection of the federal president and the vice-president, (4) the formation of a federal cabinet, (5) drawing up a federal budget, (6) formation of a federal defense force, and (7) the establishment of a federal parliament.[6] In retrospect, the rulers who met to discuss the federation could have brought the federation to successful

---

[4] Nil, Bu'rat al-Khatar, pp. 255-261.

[5] A settlement was reached between Saudi Arabia and Abu Dhabi over the Buraimi Oasis in August 1974. *Washington Post*, 22 August 1974.

[6] Nil, Bu'rat al-Khatar, pp. 122-123. See also al-Rayyis, *Sira' al-Wahat wa al-Naft*, pp. 43-57 and Salim al-Lawzi, *Rasasatan fi al-Khalij* [Two Bullets in the Gulf] (Beirut, Lebanon: al-Hawadith Publications, 1971).

fruition, especially since they were not accountable to their people nor did they need to justify any of their actions to any party in their amirates.

A primary factor that contributed to the failure of the politics of federation was the refusal of both Saudi Arabia and Iran, the two largest states of the gulf, to endorse the whole idea of a federation. Kuwaiti mediation on behalf of the federation notwithstanding, King Faisal made it clear at the time that he would not recognize any federation under the leadership of Shaikh Zayid of Abu Dhabi. Across the gulf, Iran made it even clearer that once British forces left the gulf by the end of 1971, Iran would reactivate its claims over the sovereignty of Bahrain.

It was obvious that Iran used the Bahraini question for bargaining purposes; it wanted a foothold in the gulf off its shores. Bahrain took the Iranian claim seriously and was willing to enter into negotiation with Iran, negotiations that were pushed forward by Saudi Arabia, the United States, the United Kingdom, and later the United Nations secretary-general. Therefore Bahrain helped to scuttle the federation and became independent on 14 August 1971.[7] On 30 November of the same year Iranian troops occupied the three islands of Abu Musa, the Greater Tunb and the Lesser Tunb in the gulf. The occupation was mildly protested by the Arab gulf states, but it remains in effect.

Although the politics of federation failed in 1968–1971, the idea of Arab unity along the lines of a federation remains alive among the now independent states. Curiously enough, Saudi Arabia would now support a federated state on its eastern border, which would include the original seven amirates of the United Arab Emirates plus Bahrain and Qatar. Iran also would not be opposed to such a federation, provided the present conservative political ideology continues to prevail.[8]

In addition to the politics of federation, the Arab gulf states have been occupied with the politics of radicalism. In the context of the gulf's tribal regimes, radicalism could be one of many demands: political reform, labor unions, individual rights, popular participation in government, the right to dissent. It also obviously means rejection of the existing political status quo and the attempt to change it utilizing all available means, including violent revolution. Radicalism,

---

[7] For the story of Bahrain's independence and the United Nations's role in it see *Report of the Personal Representative of the Secretary-General in Charge of the Good Offices Mission, Bahrain* (S/9772) and United Nations Security Council, *Resolution 287 (1970).*

[8] Ramazani, *The Persian Gulf: Iran's Role,* pp. 88-118.

synonymously referred to as the Arab left, is an essential ingredient in gulf politics, of which regional diplomacy must always be cognizant. Leftist ideology in the gulf may be analyzed in terms of five models: the Iraqi model, the Kuwaiti model, the Bahraini model, the South Yemeni model, and the revolutionary model. The first four models have operated within the present state system while the fifth, represented primarily by the PFLO operates outside the existing state system.

The Iraqi model revolves around the Ba'thist regime in Iraq which came to power in 1963 following the end of the Qasim regime that had ruled Iraq since the overthrow of the Hashimite monarchy in 1958. The Iraqi model professes a socialist system of government in which the Ba'th party acts as the vanguard of social transformation. Aside from its almost constant boundary disputes with Iran in the Shatt al-'Arab area [9] and its territorial disputes with Kuwait, Iraq has had to deal with the Kurdish problem at home. Ideologically, the Iraqi model has little to offer to the lower gulf regimes or even their political elites. Iraqi Ba'thists have not been able to build any ideological bridge to the political elite down the gulf. The Iraqis have supported the PFLO and other revolutionary movements, especially those directed against the shah's regime in Iran. Internationally, Iraq has established warm relations, economic and political, with the Soviet Union and India, and it has been a link in a vague Soviet-Iraqi-Indian relationship in the gulf. Generally speaking, Iraq has suffered from three constraints: (1) diplomatic isolation from its neighbors, (2) the lack of a deep-water port on the gulf, and (3) shaky internal political stability.[10]

The Kuwaiti leftist model is somewhat unique in the gulf. Although it is a family-ruled amirate and one of the world's richest states, Kuwait is the first gulf amirate to adopt a constitution and to establish a popularly elected parliament. By this experiment, the al-Sabah ruling family has expressed a desire to share a portion of its authority with the Kuwaiti people. The twelve-year constitutional experiment in Kuwait has worked relatively well. The left in Kuwait has developed and continues to function within the system. What is important here is that, regardless of its rhetoric in parliament and the ideological labels by which certain factions of the Kuwaiti left identify themselves, it has functionally accepted the legitimacy of the Kuwaiti family-ruled regime and of the system of government.

---

[9] Majid Khadduri, ed., *Major Middle Eastern Problems in International Law* (Washington, D. C.: American Enterprise Institute for Public Policy Research, 1972), pp. 88-94.

[10] *The Arabian Peninsula*, p. 47.

No political parties exist in Kuwait so far, and the constitution is ambivalent on this question. The recent national debates on whether political parties should be permitted, however, have revealed the existence of three main ideological groupings in the country with representation in the National Assembly.[11] First, a Marxist bloc headed by Ahmad al-Khatib, a member of the National Assembly, has called for nationalization of the oil industry and a radical systemic change in Kuwaiti society. Second, a nationalist bloc headed by Jasim al-Qatami, a member of the National Assembly and a former leader of the Arab Nationalists' Movement, has called for close cooperation with the Nasserist ideology and support of the democratic experiment in Kuwait. The third bloc is the liberal democrats, a right-wing group headed by Hamad al-'Isa, also a member of the National Assembly. This group has strongly attacked the left and is a staunch supporter of the Kuwaiti regime. Of the three, the Marxist (but not necessarily Communist) bloc is the most organized. It publishes a weekly and occupies several seats in the National Assembly.[12]

Leftist ideology in Bahrain has been represented recently in a bloc called the "People's Coalition," of which eight candidates were elected members of the National Assembly in December 1973.[13] Like their Kuwaiti counterparts, members of the Bahraini left have so far worked within the newly established constitutional system. They have of course called for political reform on all levels of government. Unlike the Kuwaiti groups, however, the left in Bahrain has a long tradition of activity in which laborers and intellectuals have worked together. The Bahraini left has addressed its activities to the social and economic conditions inside Bahrain.

The political stratum in Bahrain has generally been urbane, civil and politically sophisticated. This group has also included political leaders, and it has always worked toward political reform and demanded more individual rights and freedoms. The participation of the Bahraini left in the election to the National Assembly, despite the calls from the radical left for a boycott of the election, demonstrated its willingness to give the constitutional experiment a chance and its

---

[11] For an interesting discussion of this point see an article entitled "Will Political Parties Enter the Gulf Through Kuwait?" in *Sada al-'Usbu'* (Bahrain), 4 June 1974, pp. 14-15.

[12] Ibid.

[13] See *al-Tali'a*, 12 December 1973; *al-Adwa'*, 13 December 1973; *Sada al-'Usbu'*, 15 December 1973; and *Akhbar al-Bahrain*, 10 December 1973 (a special issue on the election results). The original leader of the group, Dr. 'Abd al-Hadi Khalaf, was later ordered by the courts to relinquish his seat because he had falsified his age in order to qualify for the election. (*al-Adwa'*, 7 February 1974).

ability to learn from previous mistakes.[14] The Bahraini left has concentrated its efforts on the problem of the working class in the country. The labor strikes in 1973 and 1974 are a pointed indication that labor is the primary national issue, and the left, as well as many other political elements in the society, has long realized that radical social change would only come through the Bahraini laborer.

On the regional level, the Bahraini left has spoken out against Iranian hegemony in the region, condemned the Bahraini-American agreement for home-porting facilities at Jufair, supported the Dhufar rebellion and the Palestine revolution and called for a more effective use of the oil weapon against Western, primarily American, interests. Some extremely radical elements of the left who have participated in labor strikes and actively called for labor strikes against either government or Western businesses have frequently been imprisoned; others have been exiled. This means that the issue of labor unions and the right to unionize would continue to make the position of Western firms in Bahrain tenuous for some time to come unless the Bahraini government can find a workable solution. The active interest with which some gulf and foreign governments followed the Bahraini election in December 1973 and the concern which these governments expressed over the victory of the leftist bloc in the election underscores the fact that domestic politics is a major support of diplomacy in the gulf. In responding to the flood of analyses and reportorial comment about the election, the prime minister said, "It seems as if the future of democracy in the Arab world is going to be decided in Manama."[15]

The socialist regime in the People's Democratic Republic of Yemen (PDRY) has also influenced gulf diplomacy. This regime is the fourth model of the Arab left in the region, and it is a unique case in that it is the first, and thus far the only, socialist regime in the Arabian Peninsula. It came to power in November 1967 when the British government granted the former Aden protectorate its independence. The National Liberation Front, under the leadership of Qahtan al-Sha'bi, led the war for the liberation of Aden, and after independence it assumed the affairs of state. Two years later (June 1969) al-Sha'bi was removed and was replaced by a presidential council. Since then the PDRY has deepened its commitment to a socialist course of national development.

---

[14] The radical left was strongly criticized by many Bahrainis for refusal to participate in the 1972 election to the Constitutional Assembly.

[15] al-Bahrain al-Yom, 12 August 1974, p. 9. For a special analysis of the election see al-Anwar (Beirut), 16 December 1973, pp. 6-7.

During the last half decade, the socialist regime of PDRY has radically changed the entire society and has removed all vestiges—administrative, political, economic—of the country's tribal past.[16] The National Liberation Front, PDRY's only legal political party, has institutionalized its ideology in the new state along the lines of a left-wing socialist republic. The PDRY's ideological orientation is perhaps the most radical in the Arab world, and it is not surprising that the conservative regimes in the Arabian peninsula and along the gulf littoral have eyed PDRY's socialism with grave concern. Saudi Arabia is reported to have financially supported certain Yemeni dissident elements to overthrow the socialist regime in Aden.[17]

Diplomatically, PDRY is relatively isolated from its neighbors, and it has actively and staunchly supported the rebellion in Dhufar against the Qabus regime in Oman. Iraq is the only country in the region with which PDRY has maintained warm relations. On the international level, PDRY has established close relations with countries of the Eastern bloc, particularly East Germany. Its relations with the West have been cool. The fact that a socialist regime could establish itself in the Arabian Peninsula in the form of a sovereign and internationally recognized state has given regional diplomacy an added dimension which must not be ignored.

The PFLO and its Dhufari rebellion [18] together constitute the political activity that is by far the most disturbing to gulf leaders. The radical ideology of the PFLO, which represents the revolutionary model of the Arab left, is so far the only ideology that has opted for violence to bring about a desired political change. The popular front has concluded that it could not coexist with the tribal autocratic regime of the Sultanate of Oman and has therefore set out to change that status quo by revolution. What concerns us here is the tremendous direct impact this rebellion has had on regional and international diplomacy. Until very recently, the PFLO has been supported by China and the Soviet Union and, on the local level, by the PDRY. Ideologically, it has also been supported by small groups of leftists scattered throughout the gulf.

---

16 *Area Handbook*, pp. 65-94 and *The Arabian Peninsula*, pp. 51-54.

17 *The Arabian Peninsula*, p. 52. The ideological dispute between North Yemen and PDRY remains a source of potential conflict in that part of the Arabian Peninsula. Saudi Arabia and Kuwait, and more recently Syria and the Palestine Liberation Organization, have in recent months attempted to resolve the conflict between the Yemens through mediation.

18 For a close look into conditions in Dhufar see *al-Tali'a*, 2 February 1974, pp. 15-18.

In terms of regional politics, the PFLO has been a link in a Chinese-Yemeni (PDRY)-PFLO relationship in the region. On the Indian subcontinent this axis is complemented by Pakistan. In a rather vague way, it has paralleled the Indian-Iraqi-Soviet axis. Both Iraq and the Soviet Union, however, have supported the Dhufari rebellion. The Soviet Union did not lock itself into a pro-Iraqi posture; it has been able to conclude huge commercial agreements with Iran for natural gas. More recently, it has established friendly relations with Kuwait, Iraq's neighbor at Shatt al-'Arab. To counteract China's support of Pakistan, the Soviet Union has in the last two years supported the Baluchi National Liberation Movement (BNLM) whose avowed goal is to liberate Baluchistan,[19] a territory located on the border separating Iran and Pakistan.[20] The BNLM, whose activities are directed against the Iranian and Pakistani regimes, has opened an office in Iraq. The Soviet Union, however, has not allowed its support for the Baluchi movement to disturb its commercial relations with Iran. More recently, Soviet diplomatic activities in the gulf have indicated a new tendency on the part of the Soviet government: the desire to deal with established states, including Kuwait and Saudi Arabia.

Superpower détente has also led to a change in Chinese diplomacy. The fallout of this change has been felt in the gulf, particularly in the changing Chinese attitude toward the PFLO. The first public indication of Chinese diplomacy in the gulf came with the three-day visit of China's foreign minister, Chi Peng-Fei, to Teheran in June 1973. The Chinese-Iranian rapprochement was allegedly designed by the Chinese to counteract the Soviet influence in the gulf, centered in Baghdad. Not only did Chinese and Russian support of the PFLO decrease, but by the end of 1973, the advent of parliamentary constitutionalism in Bahrain and the almost total participation of the Bahraini left-wing in the national election left the PFLO with no active followers or supporters outside Oman. Bahrain was a serious blow to the popular front because the sophisticated Bahraini left and the relatively advanced level of political consciousness among the country's political elites were always viewed by front leadership as a susceptible target for political action.

Another adverse development from the front's viewpoint was Iranian military participation in the sultan's fight against the Dhufari

---

[19] For a close look into Baluchi conditions see a special report on Baluchistan in al-Tali'a, 1 December 1973, pp. 15-17.

[20] According to recent estimated statistics, the Baluchis in Pakistan, Iran and Afghanistan total over 7 million people, 30 percent of whom live in Pakistan. Ibid., p. 15.

rebellion. The landing of Iranian troops in Oman in December 1973 was treated with complete official silence in the neighboring Arab countries. A third recent development has been the cooling of relations between the PFLO and the National Liberation Front in Aden. Simply stated, the PDRY regime has embarked on a new campaign to end its isolation. Like Moscow and Peking, Aden too has felt the warmth of détente and has begun a new attempt to deal with its neighbors on a state-to-state basis. This change in the PDRY's attitude toward its neighbors is by and large due to the quiet, relentless Kuwaiti diplomacy of the past year to create a limited détente among the sister Arab states of the gulf.[21]

Based on these developments, the PFLO decided in August 1974 to remove "and the Arabian Gulf" from its title and to concentrate its efforts on the rebellion in Dhufar. In its statement announcing the change in name, the popular front said that "the present situation dictates that all national forces must be united and secondary disagreements must be resolved in order to face the Iranian invaders, defeat them and then bring down the client regime in the Sultanate of Muscat." [22]

In terms of gulf diplomacy, the front's recognition of the "new reality" is not and must not be taken as a sign that the age of revolution is over in the region. The need for political reform within the different regimes is imperative. In fact, political oppression and autocracy in years past were precisely the factors that precipitated this rebellion. The degree and nature of political reform and development will remain significant factors in gulf diplomacy for years to come.

Another aspect of the Arab presence in the gulf is the Palestine conflict and the type of attitude which the region's governments have maintained toward the Palestine question as an Arab national issue and toward the Palestine revolution as the voice of the Palestinians. In terms of population, there are nearly 200,000 Palestinians in Kuwait, approximately 10,000 in each of Qatar and the United Arab Emirates and about 2,000 in Bahrain.[23] In terms of influence, Palestinians hold hundreds of very high civil service positions in Kuwait, Qatar, and the individual amirates of the United Arab Emirates. They manage private businesses ranging from restaurants to printshops to banks. One important example of their political importance in

---

[21] *Sada al-'Usbu'*, 13 August 1974, p. 8.

[22] Ibid.

[23] These figures are based on approximate estimates of several government officials in these countries. One difficulty facing statisticians in this case is the fact that thousands of Palestinians carry Jordanian citizenship, which means that at least officially they are considered Jordanian nationals.

terms of the Palestinian question is the fact that in several amirates Palestinians virtually run both the educational systems and the information departments. Moreover, the Palestine revolution makes its presence felt through Fateh offices in Kuwait, Qatar (a regional office for the lower gulf), Bahrain and Saudi Arabia. The rulers of the Arab gulf states contribute substantially to the Palestine cause.

The October War and the Arab oil embargo against the United States and Holland, Israel's closest friends in the West, clearly indicated that Palestine is an issue still very much alive in the gulf. In fact, King Faisal's adamant position during the oil embargo even surprised many Palestinians. Prior to the October War, the Palestine conflict in the Arab world was primarily confined within the "confrontation" states of Egypt, Syria, Jordan, and Lebanon. The support frequently voiced by Arab leaders beyond the confrontation circle was often merely rhetorical, and the Arab gulf was no exception. The traditional position of Arab gulf states on Palestine, that is, oil and politics do not mix, was the basis of regional and international relations for almost a generation. The October War, however, has sounded a new note: no relations, political or economic, between the Arab states and foreign powers can be expected to endure unless the Palestine conflict is finally resolved. Such a position can ultimately affect the United States more than any other country.

As a major backer of the Egyptian military effort during the October War and of the Egyptian postwar recovery program, Saudi Arabia has become more deeply involved in the Arab-Israeli conflict in Palestine than ever before. This new, direct Saudi involvement spells potential trouble for the United States, assuming the conflict is prolonged, especially since Saudi Arabia has become the world's largest producer of oil. Simply stated, the Palestinian issue has invaded the gulf on a large scale, and diplomacy in the area will be affected by it so long as the conflict is not resolved. Even if certain gulf Arab leaders would like to wish it out of existence, events in the last year have shown that the politics of Palestine have penetrated the economics of oil to the very core.

Regional Diplomacy: Iranian Hegemony

The Iranian presence constitutes the second sphere of gulf diplomacy. The shah had made it known as early as 1968 that following the British withdrawal, the region's stability and security was to be henceforth preserved by Iranian military might. *Pax Persiana* was to replace *Pax Britannica*. With the approval of the Western powers, especially the United States, the shah proceeded to establish himself as the defender of the peace in the gulf and to amass by far the largest arms arsenal in the history of the region.[24] The shah argued that this was necessary to fill the political/ideological vacuum which would follow the British withdrawal and make the gulf an inviting target for outside powers and influences.

The shah's view of Iran's role in the gulf has generally been accepted in the United States, and it has been felt that his use of American technology (weapons) would be a sure formula for regional stability.[25] The shah has argued that Iran's military superiority in the gulf would be a credible deterrence against any possible outside aggression. The United States has so far supported this position. Any reassessment of American long-range policy in the region, however, would almost have to include a redefinition of the nature and source of this potential "aggression." Such a step would hopefully save the United States from getting involved in a nightmare of inter-regime and intra-regime conflicts which would be suppressed under the pretense of repelling aggression.

Iran sees its new posture as serving at least three main objectives: to protect the regime against subversion, regardless of whether the source is internal or from the outside; to guarantee free shipping in the gulf; and to protect Iran's oil resources and facilities.[26] The realization of those objectives, the shah has argued, would also serve American interests, and the United States seems to have accepted this proposition.

The application of this theory of deterrence has led Iran to adopt a twofold strategy: the buildup of a credible military machine and the pursuit of an active diplomacy. The military presence has been demonstrated by a visible military force and a visible military action. Underlying all of this is the personal leadership of the shah.

The concerted buildup of Iran's new armed forces began after 1968 and has accelerated at an astonishing pace. The United States has been a primary source of weapons. The ominous implications of this development, the effectiveness of the shah's military might as a deterrent and the potential U.S. involvement in the gulf have increas-

---

[24] For an excellent analysis of the unprecedented military buildup in the gulf, see Dale R. Tahtinen, *Arms in the Persian Gulf* (Washington, D. C.: American Enterprise Institute for Public Policy Research, 1974).

[25] "America and the Middle East," *The Annals*, vol. 401 (May 1972), a special issue edited by former Ambassador Parker T. Hart. See especially pp. 106-115. See also Koury, *Oil and Geopolitics*, pp. 35-54.

[26] *The Arabian Peninsula*, p. 22.

ingly become the focus of debate in Washington.[27] The Iranian navy presently boasts destroyers, minesweepers, landing craft, air-cushion vehicles, patrol ships and war ships. The army and air force also possess some of the world's most sophisticated weapons systems. The Iranian military is fast becoming a significant force, and the qualitative and quantitative superiority of the Iranian armed forces becomes strikingly evident when compared to the two largest Arab states in the region, Iraq and Saudi Arabia. Although the 1973–1974 military statistics in Table 3 do not reflect the procurement of weapons by the states involved since the October War, the picture of Iran's military superiority is not likely to change in the foreseeable future.[28] The military capability of the other Arab gulf states—the amirates— which is presently being updated, is rather minuscule (see note to Table 3). This is yet another indication that Iran's military hegemony will continue for many years to come.

For his country's military deterrence to be effective, the shah believes that Iran's military capability must be both visible and active. Arab diplomacy in the region has again felt Iran's determination in this area. Not only are Iranian warships constantly visible in the Indian Ocean and the gulf, but Iran conducted a significant naval operation in full view of the Arab states, one which directly concerned them.[29] This operation occurred on 30 November 1971 when the Iranian navy stormed the three gulf islands of Abu Musa and the two Tunbs. The timing of this operation was significant in that December 1971 signaled the dismantling of the British military presence in the area. On 2 December the United Arab Emirates was formed as an independent state. Ra's al-Khayma joined the United Arab Emirates on 11 February 1972.

From a regional perspective, the shah's naval operation against Abu Musa and the Tunbs underscored at least three points:

(1) He was on his way to becoming a leader of international stature.

(2) He made it clear to his neighbors that he considered Iranian military hegemony a serious matter.

(3) He was intent on establishing this hegemony through every means at his disposal, military and diplomatic, Arab protests notwithstanding. The active diplomacy that preceded the operation was conducted on many levels and involved many states and parties: Iran,

---

[27] See Tahtinen, *Arms in the Persian Gulf.*

[28] For a close look at Iran's air power and ground and naval forces, see ibid., pp. 2-18.

[29] Iran's military operation in Oman is another illustration of this point.

England, Sharja and Ra's al-Khayma (later members of the United Arab Emirates). Diplomacy also involved the United States and several Arab countries.

The British Special Envoy, Sir William Luce, a former political resident in the gulf (1961–1966), played a very active diplomatic role during the final days of British presence in the region, especially during the latter months of 1971. By the end of that year, a consensus had developed among the United States, England and Iran over at least five basic principles for long-range diplomacy in the gulf:

(1) The independence of the newly emerging Arab political entities would be protected.

(2) Free access by the West to gulf oil would be maintained.

(3) Political stability, based on conservative state ideologies, would be necessary for the free flow of oil.

(4) Radicalism in any form, states or movements, would not be welcomed or tolerated.

(5) Iranian diplomatic and military hegemony would remain a principal guarantor of stability in the region.

Goals and Options: The Arab Gulf States

Arab gulf diplomacy, as was pointed out above, is often influenced by factors outside the region itself, and therefore it is designed to achieve many goals. Although these goals are primarily gulf-centered, they also concern two other, equally important, areas: the Arab world and the international community. These goals might vary from state to state, and in a narrow sense one cannot speak of collective goals. On a wider plane, however, one must realize that these states, conservative or radical, are interconnected by very deep bonds: Islam, language, history, oil, geographic proximity and, above all, Arabism ('uruba). Such phrases as "Arab brotherhood" and "Arab unity," which to outsiders seem to be empty clichés, are lodged deep in the Arab psyche. They are prime movers in the process of selecting national goals.

Long-range goals of the Arab gulf states may be divided into three categories: regional goals, Arab/national goals and international goals. On the regional level political stability is the overriding goal, but the Arab states, including Saudi Arabia, reject the shah of Iran's self-assumed role of gulf policeman. Arab elites and media have in the last two years often expressed certain fears of Iran's territorial ambitions. These fears have a three-pronged base:

Table 3

MAJOR WEAPONS AND MILITARY PERSONNEL IN THE GULF AREA

	Iran	Iraq	Saudi Arabia	Kuwait
Army				
Personnel	175,000	100,000	36,000	8,000
Tanks				
Chieftain	300 (480 on order)			
M-47	400			
M-60 A1	460		25	
Scorpion	(250 on order)			
T-62		1,300*		
T-54/55				
T-34				
PT-76		90		
AMX-30			30 (150 on order)	
M-41			60	
AML-60				
AML-90				
Vickers				50
Centurion			200	50
Total tanks	1,160 (730 on order)	1,390*	315 (150 on order)	100
Armored Personnel Carriers				
M-113	2,000*			
BTR-50				
BTR-60				

BTR-60 }				
BMP-76 }		1,300*		
BTR-152 }				
Total armored personnel carriers	2,000*	1,300*		2,000
Air Force				
Personnel	50,000	10,500	5,500	
Combat Aircraft				
F-4D	32			
F-4E with Sidewinder & Sparrow AAM	64 (70 on order)			
F-5A	100			
SU-7		60		
F-14	(80 on order)			
F-28	(4 on order)			
F-5E			14	
F-5B	(141 on order)			
F-5E/B			20 (126 on order)	
MiG-17		30		
Mirage IIIESA			(38 on order)	
Tu-16		8		
RF-4E	4			
RF-5A	16			
Hunter		20	21 (9 on order)	
BAC-167			35	
F-52/F-53				12 (20 on order)
Mirage F1				
MiG-21		100		
P-3 Orion	(6 on order)			28 (20 on order)
Total combat aircraft	216 (301 on order)	218*	90 (173 on order)	

Table 3 (Continued)

Helicopters	Iran	Iraq	Saudi Arabia	Kuwait
AB-206			20	
AB-205			10	
AB-204			1	
Alouette III		20	6	
AB-206A	43			
AB-212	5			
CH-47C	18 (22 on order)			
Huskie	32			
Mi-4		35		
Mi-6		16		
Mi-8		30		
UH-IH/214 Huey Plus	(287 on order)			
AB-204B				6
Whirlwind				1
Gazelle				(20 on order)
AB-205A	4 (52 on order)			
SH-3D	10			
Puma				(10 on order)
Total helicopters	112 (361 on order)	101	37	7 (30 on order)

44

Navy

Personnel	13,000	2,000	1,500	200
Destroyers	3			
Frigates with MK 2 Seakiller SSM and Seacat SAM	4			
Corvettes	4			
Patrol Boats	10	6	20	10
Osa-class with Styx SSM		3		
Minesweepers	6	2		
Landing Craft	4			2
Hovercraft				
SRN-6	8		8	
Wellington BH-N7	2			
	(2 on order)			
	(6 on order)			
Fast Patrol Boats Jaguar class			4	
SOI Submarine Chasers		3		
P-6 Torpedo Boats		12		
Patrol Launches				8
Total	41	26	32	20
	(8 on order)			

* Approximate.

Note: Additional forces in the gulf area include: Abu Dhabi—6 patrol boats, 10 Mirage (4 on order), 8 Hunter aircraft and 13 helicopters; Bahrain—2 scout helicopters; Qatar—4 Hunter aircraft and 2 Whirlwind helicopters; Dubai—2 AB-206 helicopters.

Source: *The Military Balance 1974–1975* (London: The International Institute for Strategic Studies, 1974).

45

(1) Iran's occupation of Abu Musa and the Tunbs in November 1971 and the landing of Iranian troops in Oman in December 1973.

(2) The extensive and costly buildup of the Iranian armed forces, especially the navy and air force, in recent years.

(3) The often-repeated statements of Iranian officials pointing out the shah's ordained role as the protector of "60% of the world's oil."[30]

The Arab littoral states and Iran agree on the regional security goal; they disagree sharply on the means.

There are some interesting questions which are now being asked by the Arab states. Why does the shah need such a military machine? If Iran feels insecure on its northern frontier with the Soviet Union, why would it concentrate on its naval buildup? Can the shah ever really hope to create a credible military capability against the Soviet Union? Or is this military machine designed to spread the Iranian view of regional stability over both sides of the gulf and to maintain the type of ideological purity which is to the shah's liking? Could the shah be engaged in some contingency planning which would, future situations permitting, include an Iranian occupation of oil resources on the Arab side of the gulf?[31] A major psychological motive underlying Arab fears of Iranian dominance in the gulf is a reaction to the presence of relatively large Iranian minorities in all of the amirates, principally in the commercial sector. These minorities have not assimilated into the societies in which they live; they stubbornly maintain their national identity in language, culture and, many Arabs allege, in national aspirations.

Frequent calls have been issued for the Bahrainization, Qatarization, general Arabization of this sector throughout the Arab gulf in recent years. Similar calls have been heard concerning the Indian minority, especially in Bahrain.[32] This aspect of regional stability and security has a special meaning to gulf Arabs: they desire regional security but not under an Iranian umbrella.

The other side of the regional security coin gives a different picture. The conservative Arab gulf states are deeply suspicious of Soviet long-range designs on the gulf. They are wary of the cozy relationship between the Soviet Union and India, with Iraq as the fulcrum of this axis in the gulf. Again, gulf Arabs take note of the presence of large Indian minorities in their midst. Added to this is

---

[30] *Sada al-'Usbu'*, 11 June 1974, p. 6. A special article entitled "Arab-Iranian Relations: The Beginning and the End," pp. 6-8.

[31] Ibid.

[32] For a recent example see *Sada al-'Usbu'*, 20 August 1974, p. 7. The Bahrainization of labor has been a politically sensitive issue on the island for years.

the Muslim Arab's deep-seated distrust of communism. Gulf Arabs generally agree that Soviet strategy toward the gulf is threefold:

(1) Ensure that the gulf does not become involved in any Western-supported security alliances whose ultimate purpose would be to block any future expansion of Soviet interests southward.

(2) Use the gulf as a springboard for the expansion of Soviet presence and influence in the Indian Ocean.

(3) Maintain open access to gulf oil and gas.[33]

In addition to regional security and stability, another important national goal for gulf Arabs is continued free international trade, especially shipping. International shipping constitutes the lifeline of Arab gulf states. They export their oil and import practically all of their needs. The unhindered flow of international trade, which usually indicates a relatively stable international economy, is essential for the economic well-being of the region. To illustrate, in 1972 the Arab gulf states imported goods valued at almost 4 billion dollars. In the same year, their corrected oil revenues were over 6 billion dollars.

In terms of Arab national issues the primary goal of the Arab gulf states is, according to their official statements, the resolution of the Palestine conflict and the restoration of legitimate national rights to the Palestinian people. Like many other Arab states, however, the gulf states have not formed a united position on the means to be employed for resolving the conflict. Indeed, Arab unity, at least a unity of purpose if not of governments and states, has been another major Arab national goal. Finally, on the international level, the Arab gulf states have sought a strong United Nations and an internationally recognized legal system.

In order to achieve the above goals, the Arab gulf states have several avenues available to them. On the regional level, at least five possibilities present themselves:

(1) Frequent high-level contacts between the states themselves.

(2) The possibility of settling outstanding territorial and other disputes with Iran, thereby paving the way for warmer relations between the two littorals of the gulf.

(3) The possible emergence of Saudi Arabia as a major gulf power that could rally the support of the neighboring Arab states for any future regional security arrangements, something that Iran has, for various reasons, failed to do.

(4) The development of a long-range plan for economic cooperation, which could produce gulf shipping lines, unified trade policies,

---

[33] Ibid., p. 11.

complementary industrial policies and ultimately a full-fledged technological society.

(5) The continued discussion among themselves of the need for future political reform, especially since the Kuwaiti and Bahraini constitutional experiments have proven somewhat successful.

In the final analysis, real security can only develop when the gap of suspicion and distrust between the people and their government is closed and when the people are invited to participate in the affairs of their new state.

On Arab national issues, the Arab gulf states have other possibilities available to them:

(1) Support of United Nations resolutions on Palestine.

(2) Support of American-Arab peace efforts on Palestine.

(3) Support of Egyptian and Syrian disengagement agreements with Israel.

(4) Support of the Palestine Liberation Organization and its recently adopted stand favoring an interim territorial solution, that is, the establishment of a Palestinian state.

(5) Financial support of the "confrontation" states, thereby enabling those states to negotiate with Israel from a position of strength.

On the international level, the options available to Arab gulf states include the following:

(1) Support of the United Nations Organization and its specialized agencies, such as the United Nations Development Program, the Food and Agriculture Organization, the International Monetary Fund, and the International Bank for Reconstruction and Development.

(2) Support of superpower détente and all efforts toward disarmament.

(3) Support of all efforts designed to keep the Indian Ocean out of superpower rivalries and the concomitant prospects of a nuclear buildup.

Recent diplomatic activities of gulf leaders [34] indicate an awareness of the options available to them and that they fully appreciate the ways in which their new-found economic power can be channeled in the service of peace, regionally and internationally.

---

[34] For example, see al-Dawha (Qatar), August 1974 for the recent visit of Qatar's ruler to the "confrontation" states; Akhbar Dubai (Dubai), 27 June 1974 for the recent visit of Dubai's ruler to India; Akhbar Dubai (Dubai), 15 August 1974 for the recent visit of the United Arab Emirates' president to Egypt and Libya; and al-Adwa' (Bahrain), 15 August 1974 for the recent exchange of visits between Saudi Arabian and Bahraini high officials.

Goals and Options: The United States

In a statement before the House Foreign Affairs Subcommittee during hearings in summer 1973, Joseph Sisco, assistant secretary of state for Near Eastern and South Asian affairs, referred to the Arab/Persian Gulf as an area in which "we have very, very significant political-economic-strategic interests." [35] Earlier in the statement, Sisco defined those interests as being:

> (1) Support for indigenous regional collective security efforts to provide stability and to foster orderly development without outside interference.
>
> (2) The peaceful resolution of territorial and other disputes among the regional states and the opening up of better channels of communication among them.
>
> (3) Continued access to Gulf oil supplies at reasonable prices and in sufficient quantities to meet our growing needs and those of our European and Asian friends and allies.
>
> (4) Enhancing of our commercial and financial interests.[36]

In the same hearings, James Noyes, deputy assistant secretary of defense for Near East, African and South Asian affairs, described United States security interests in the gulf as follows:

> (1) Containment of Soviet military power within its present borders;
>
> (2) access to Persian Gulf oil; and
>
> (3) continued free movement of United States ships and aircraft into and out of the area.[37]

These interests continue to be the focus of American relations in the gulf region.[38]

United States strategic and security interests in the gulf are based on three primary considerations: (1) the gulf as a source of oil, (2) the gulf as an extension of the Indian Ocean, and (3) the gulf as an extension of the traditional Middle East and the Arab-Israeli conflict. The United States's primary national goal has been to contain Soviet influence in the gulf, thereby insuring the free flow of

---

[35] House Committee on Foreign Affairs, *New Perspectives on the Persian Gulf*, p. 6.

[36] Ibid., p. 2.

[37] Ibid., p. 39.

[38] A statement by Seymour Weiss, director, Bureau of Politico-Military Affairs, Department of State, House Committee on Foreign Affairs, in *Proposed Expansion of U.S. Military Facilities in the Persian Gulf*, pp. 21-49.

oil to Europe and the United States, and in the Indian Ocean, thereby maintaining a pro-American balance of power in the region.

In order to realize the above goals and interests, the United States has entered into several military and economic assistance agreements with countries in the region. The options and policies pursued over the last several years have been designed to serve the following objectives:

(1) Help the countries of the region maintain their independence, stability and security.

(2) Maintain friendly relations between them and the United States and its allies.

(3) Support their orderly economic, social and political development.

(4) Help those countries provide for their defense through American military assistance.[39]

Table 4

ARMS TRANSFER PROGRAMS TO SAUDI ARABIA
(1965–1973)
(in thousands of dollars)

Year	Military Assistance Program	Excess Defense Articles [a]	Foreign Military Sales	Ship Loans	Commercial Sales [b]	Total
1965	1,263	—	6,040	—	856	8,159
1966	668	—	81,312	—	14,902	96,882
1967	768	—	94,348	—	33,580	128,696
1968	759	—	34,312	—	35,481	70,552
1969	620	—	3,947	—	6,253	10,820
1970	532	—	2,551	—	12,723	15,806
1971	640	2	73,136	—	8,200	81,978
1972	474	—	306,797	—	5,134	312,405
1973	217	—	60,693	—	(15,450) [c]	76,360

a Value in accordance with section 8(c) of Public Law 91-672.

b Deliveries.

c Estimate.

Source: *New Perspectives on the Persian Gulf*, 93d Congress, 1st Session (Washington, D. C.: U.S. Government Printing Office, 1973), p. 47.

[39] House Committee on Foreign Affairs, *New Perspectives on the Persian Gulf*, p. 39.

Table 5

ARMS TRANSFER PROGRAMS TO IRAN
(1965–1973)
(in thousands of dollars)

Year	Military Assistance Program	Excess Defense Articles [a]	Foreign Military Sales	Ship Loans	Commercial Sales [b]	Total
1965	33,547	203	59,676	—	57	93,483
1966	62,696	832	137,536	—	5,122	206,186
1967	34,690	631	213,591	—	2,022	250,934
1968	22,134	3	141,360	—	5,147	168,644
1969	23,899	197	212,138	—	10,084	246,318
1970	2,631	—	91,208	—	9,811	103,650
1971	2,090	—	445,913	—	27,059	475,062
1972	934	—	499,217	12,700	39,885	552,736
1973	—	—	2,054,311	—	(42,400) [c]	2,096,711

[a] Value in accordance with section 8(c) of Public Law 91-672.
[b] Deliveries.
[c] Estimate.
Source: *New Perspectives on the Persian Gulf*, 93d Congress, 1st session (Washington, D. C.: U.S. Government Printing Office, 1973), p. 47.

These policies have been pursued on several levels: direct military assistance, limited military presence and certain other politico-military activities. The axis of stability in the gulf, from the United States point of view, runs through Saudi Arabia and Iran. A militarily strong Iran and a militarily strong Saudi Arabia, American policy planners have argued, could act as a credible deterrent against any outside threat. American military sales, transfers and general assistance to those two countries have been impressive and profitable. Arms transfers to Iran alone between 1965 and 1973 totaled over 4 billion dollars (Tables 4 and 5). In 1973 over thirty American firms with defense-related contracts were operating in Iran and Saudi Arabia with almost 2,000 American personnel. These firms provide "a wide spectrum of assistance to the military services of the two countries primarily related to instruction, training, and maintenance

concerning the equipment purchased from the United States." [40]
Some recent estimates place the number of American defense or
defense-related personnel in Iran between 8,000 and 10,000 people.
In terms of additional pilot training, about 175 Iranian trainees and
21 Saudi trainees are presently in the United States under pilot
training programs. [41]

In addition, the United States has signed agreements with Saudi
Arabia to modernize the Saudi navy and to arm and train its national
guard units. Early in 1973 the lower gulf states, Oman and Yemen,
were declared eligible for U.S. military sales. Kuwait was placed in
that status a year earlier. [42]

American military presence in the gulf is limited to the naval
facility in Jufair leased from the Bahraini government under an
executive agreement. This Jufair agreement, which the United States
signed with Bahrain in December 1971, is the only arrangement of its
kind in the gulf. The agreement simply provides home-porting
facilities for the small MIDEASTFOR, which basically consists of a
flagship and two destroyers. [43] The Jufair agreement was a center of
controversy in the United States Senate in January 1972 when the
existence of the agreement was revealed. [44] According to the United
States Navy, the primary mission of MIDEASTFOR has been to
conduct friendly visits to the countries of the region. When the
controversy erupted in Washington and in the Arab press in January
1972, the foreign minister of Bahrain described the agreement as
being purely commercial, and he assured the press that the agreement
would not encroach on Bahrain's independence and sovereignty. [45]
On 20 October 1973, as a result of the October War, Bahrain abruptly
terminated the agreement and asked the American navy to dismantle
its presence within a year. It is expected that Bahrain will rescind its

---

[40] Ibid., p. 57. In Iran the firms include: Boeing, Raytheon, Bowen-McLaughlin-York, Control Data Corporation, IT&T, Hughes Aircraft, Lockheed Aircraft Corporation, Northrop, Bell Helicopter, Motorola, Inc., Standwick Corporation, General Electric, Westinghouse, Philco-Ford, McDonnell-Douglas and Computer Sciences. In Saudi Arabia the firms include: Lockheed, Raytheon, Bendix, AVCO and Northrop.

[41] House Committee on Foreign Affairs, *Proposed Expansion of U.S. Military Facilities in the Indian Ocean*, p. 75. For updated information on this question, see Tahtinen, *Arms in the Persian Gulf*, pp. 24-26.

[42] House Committee on Foreign Affairs, *New Perspectives on the Persian Gulf*, p. 16.

[43] *Department of State Bulletin*, 28 February 1972, pp. 282-284.

[44] *New York Times*, 7 January 1972.

[45] *Sada al-'Usbu'* 11 January 1972.

order of 20 October 1973, enabling the navy to stay, but most probably at a higher rental fee.[46]

In addition to MIDEASTFOR, the United States Navy is in the process of expanding its communications base on the island of Diego Garcia in the Indian Ocean.[47] Diego Garcia is directly related to American long-range security interests in the Arab/Persian Gulf, as well as in the Indian subcontinent and South Asia (see map, page 54).

There is no doubt that the Arab/Persian Gulf is highly relevant to American security interests, economic and strategic, and that the United States cannot be oblivious to political developments in the region. The United States must examine fresh policy options which will have a more direct bearing on the orderly economic, social and political development of the individual states. Political reform can hardly be brought about by arms and military equipment, no matter how sophisticated. Public discontent is not as effectively quelled by an antiriot squad as it is by examining and removing the causes of the discontent.

Two additional options should be pursued by the United States. While remaining a source of arms for Saudi Arabia and Iran, the United States should consciously attempt to allay Arab fears of Iranian military dominance. The United States opposition to expansionism should be made clear to all parties. Second, the United States should thoroughly reassess the future usefulness of the Jufair agreement and therefore should renegotiate this agreement with this usefulness in mind. In order to thwart the rise of radicalism in the gulf, the United States should give these two options top priority.

Regional security for the United States, or for the gulf states, can be meaningful and enduring only in the context of domestic political stability in each state. Any new partnership on the regional or international level must be preceded by a domestic partnership between the government and its people. Only then can the United States hope to promote its interests in the Arab/Persian Gulf.

---

[46] The prime minister of Bahrain stated in August 1974 that since Arab-American relations have significantly improved since the October War, the resumption of the Jufair agreement is "very possible." *al-Bahrain al-Yom*, 12 August 1974, p. 13.

[47] For a detailed examination of the entire Diego Garcia question, see House Committee on Foreign Affairs, *Proposed Expansion of U.S. Military Facilities in the Indian Ocean*.

STRATEGIC LOCATION OF DIEGO GARCIA

Source: U.S. Congress, House, Committee on Foreign Affairs, Hearings, *Proposed Expansion of U.S. Military Facilities in the Indian Ocean*, 93d Congress, 2d session (1974).

3
THE ECONOMIC DIMENSION

An Overview

Oil is the one underpinning of all economic relations in the Arab/ Persian Gulf and between the gulf and the world. In terms of production, flow, prices, revenues, petrodollars, investment and the balance of trade, oil has occupied the center stage of international diplomacy for the past two years. Japanese, European and American dependence on gulf oil and the astronomical rise in the price of oil in the past twelve months have forced policy makers in the Western democracies to reexamine the direction of future relations between the oil-consuming industrial world and the oil-producing developing world. In terms of security and national interest, the United States has been particularly concerned about the potential instability, economic and political, in the region and the threat that such instability might pose to the free flow of oil.

This concern with instability has covered four areas: (1) continued access to gulf oil, (2) the method of payment for oil imports, (3) how "to induce the Gulf states to increase their oil production in the years ahead," [1] and (4) the probability of Soviet interference in the flow of oil. The newly acquired power of the oil-producing states, as members of OPEC and as individual states, which is due solely to their staggering oil revenues, their control of the "tap" and their realization that this control can be used to influence international diplomacy to effectuate certain political changes, has been the main preoccupation of American policy makers since the October War in 1973.

---

[1] *The Arabian Peninsula*, p. 10. This goal is becoming more and more difficult to realize in view of recent cuts in the oil production of Saudi Arabia, Kuwait, Libya and Venezuela. *Washington Post*, 27 August 1974.

OPEC, the Organization of Oil Producing and Exporting Countries, was founded in 1960 to coordinate and unify the oil policies of its member states and to protect their general interests. OPEC has become a strong collective bargaining body of oil-producing countries with the power to win concessions from the oil companies. Within a few years of its birth, OPEC had brought to an end the golden era of the oil companies in terms of their unquestioned, almost autocratic power to determine the oil policies of the producing countries. In fact, OPEC came into existence as a result of successive lowering of posted prices by the oil companies, especially in 1958, 1959, and 1960. It was not until January 1971 that OPEC, on behalf of "the gulf states," [2] succeeded in forcing the oil companies to negotiate with it as a representative body. Thus the 1971 Teheran agreement for the first time gave the producers a thirty-three cent rise in the posted prices with successive price increases in the succeeding years. In return, the producers agreed that during the term of the price agreement no price leapfrogging or embargoing would be practiced.[3]

The original members of OPEC were four gulf states (Iran, Iraq, Kuwait and Saudi Arabia) and Venezuela. Since then other members have been admitted: Qatar (1961), Libya and Indonesia (1962), Abu Dhabi (1967), Algeria (1969), Nigeria (1971), and Ecuador and Gabon (1973).[4] Although Bahrain is not a member, OPEC has generally concluded price agreements with the Bahrain Petroleum Company (Bapco) similar to those concluded by OPEC members.

What has given considerable concern to American policy makers is the fact that as of January 1974 OPEC countries possessed 66 percent of the world's total oil reserves; the United States possesses 5 percent (Table 6). "Never before in the history of mankind," stated a 1972 congressional report on the United States and the gulf, "have so many wealthy, industrialized, militarily powerful and large states been at the potential mercy of small, independent and potentially unstable states which will provide, for the foreseeable future, the fuel of advanced societies." [5] OPEC countries have successfully achieved at least two major objectives: an increase in government revenues per barrel of oil (posted prices plus taxes) and participation in the ownership of oil production.[6]

[2] Abu Dhabi, Iran, Iraq, Kuwait, Qatar and Saudi Arabia.

[3] *The Middle East and North Africa, 1973-1974* (London: Europa Publications Limited, 1973), pp. 67-73.

[4] Gabon was admitted as an associate member.

[5] Quoted in Congressional Quarterly, *The Middle East*, p. 27.

[6] House Committee on Foreign Affairs, *Oil Negotiations, OPEC, and the Stability of Supply*, p. 95.

Table 6

WORLD OIL PRODUCTION AND RESERVES

Major Areas and Selected Countries	Oil Production Estimated in 1973 (thousands of barrels per day)	Oil Reserves as of January 1974 (thousands of barrels)
ASIA-PACIFIC	2,245.2	15,635,040
EUROPE	395.5	15,990,500
MIDDLE EAST	21,374.1	350,162,500
Abu Dhabi	1,285.5	21,500,000
Bahrain	63.7	360,000
Dubai	223.0	2,500,000
Iran	6,000.0	60,000,000
Iraq	1,888.2	31,500,000
Israel	100.0 [a]	2,500
Kuwait	2,890.2	64,000,000
Neutral Zone [b]	507.5	17,500,000
Oman	271.9	5,250,000
Qatar	555.5	6,500,000
Saudi Arabia	7,417.9	132,000,000
Sharja [c]	—	1,500,000
Syria	105.7	7,100,000
Turkey	65.0	450,000
AFRICA	5,763.9	67,303,750
Algeria	1,035.4	7,640,000
Egypt	180.0	5,125,000
Libya	2,116.6	25,500,000
Morocco	0.9	750
Tunisia	87.0	950,000
WESTERN HEMISPHERE	16,122.0	75,764,669
Venezuela	3,370.0	14,000,000
United States	9,225.0	34,700,249
Canada	1,750.0	9,424,170
TOTAL NON-COMMUNIST	45,900.7	524,856,459
COMMUNIST WORLD	9,312.0	103,000,000
TOTAL WORLD	55,212.7	627,856,459

[a] Includes captured Sinai fields.

[b] The Neutral Zone is owned, administered and shared by Kuwait and Saudi Arabia.

[c] The ruler of Sharja announced on 18 July 1974 that Sharja had joined the oil producers' club with an average production of 60,000 b/d. *Petroleum and Industry News* (Abu Dhabi, Arabic), August 1974, pp. 28–29.

Source: Congressional Quarterly, *The Middle East: U.S. Policy, Israel, Oil and the Arabs* (Washington, D. C.: Congressional Quarterly Service, 1974), p. 27.

In addition to OPEC the United States has since 1968 been faced with a totally Arab oil organization called the Organization of Arab Petroleum Exporting Countries (OAPEC) which was formed by Saudi Arabia, Kuwait and Libya. The present membership also includes Algeria, Bahrain, Egypt, Iraq, Qatar, Syria and the United Arab Emirates. Although the goals and objectives of OAPEC supplement those of OPEC, OAPEC was established basically to relate Arab oil supplies to oil trade policies. It has concerned itself primarily with Arab issues and their relationship to oil. The October 1973 Arab oil embargo against the United States, among other countries, was coordinated by OAPEC.

In terms of the Arab gulf states, American policy makers have been confronted by several crucial questions: how will these states use their oil-generated influence and to what end? If they decide to use their financial capability to exercise influence, what would be the United States response? What price can the United States pay for gulf oil, in terms of money and the willingness to be influenced? [7] How can the United States alter its foreign policy to reflect American acknowledgment of the existence of the new oil power? Can the Arab states be pursuaded to reinvest their petrodollars in American trade and economy? Unfortunately, clearly defined answers to some of these questions have not been fully formulated, and the net result is that American long-range policy in the region is still as choppy as the waters of the gulf.

Oil: Economics and Politics

In a lead article in the Business and Finance Section of the *New York Times* a provocative question was raised about "how Arabs turn oil into armaments." [8] The article speculated on the possibility of Arab investments of petrodollars in the American defense industry and discussed how to prepare for, or possibly prevent, such an eventuality. Only a few years ago such a topic would have been as unthinkable as Jules Verne's voyage to the moon.

In the last two years, the world of oil has witnessed dramatic changes in production, consumption and revenues which have not been seen since the Persian government granted the first oil concession to W. K. D'Arcy, an Australian, in 1901. In the last three-

---

[7] For an excellent discussion of power and influence in international relations, see K. J. Holsti, *International Politics: A Framework for Analysis*, 2d ed. (Englewood Cliffs, New Jersey: Prentice-Hall, Inc., 1972), pp. 154-168.

[8] *New York Times*, 25 August 1974, Section 3.

quarters of a century and especially since World War II, oil from the Middle East, gulf oil in particular, has fired the engines of the modern industrial revolution across Europe, Japan and the United States. In terms of growth, the economies of the Western world have reached their present stages of maturity and high mass consumption [9] with the aid of oil, which has basically meant that real affluence on the individual level, real income per head, has been attained by the use of energy generated by oil. The oil companies, traditionally West European and American, have realized huge profits over the years, and the producing countries, until very recently, sold their oil at very low prices. For decades the producing countries were bound by the concessions agreements which they had signed with the companies. Such agreements covered "the granting of rights for research, extraction, export and sale of petroleum, the exclusive rights to build pipelines, immunity from taxes and customs dues, and the payment of royalties." [10] In addition, oil companies began to set the price of oil.

After the first successful Iranian drilling in 1908, several concessions were obtained in the 1920s and 1930s by major companies (notably Exxon, Standard Oil of California, Texaco, Gulf and Mobil) in Iraq, Bahrain, Saudi Arabia, Kuwait, and Qatar. Bahrain was the first to drill for oil (1932) in the lower gulf. Since then many new companies and consortia of companies have been formed. The increase in exploration and production and the increase in world demand swelled profits which in turn stimulated the demand for concessions.

In the intervening years several interesting developments have occurred. First, as the producing countries became more sophisticated in the business of oil, they began to question the whole basis of the concessions and the "quasi-colonial authority" [11] of the oil companies. The 1950s and 1960s witnessed new negotiations and more aggressive attitudes on the part of the oil governments vis-à-vis the companies. Not all negotiations were amicable: Mexico nationalized its concessionaire in 1938; Iran did so in 1951. But with the fall of Mossadegh in 1953, Iran was forced to compromise. Another form of negotiation, profit-sharing on a fifty-fifty basis, was introduced in 1950, first in the gulf by Saudi Arabia, then by Iraq and Kuwait. The frequent disagreements between Iraq and its concessionaire, the Iraq Petroleum Company, led finally to complete nationalization by the government

---

[9] W. W. Rostow, *The Stages of Economic Growth: A Non-Communist Manifesto*, 2d ed. (Cambridge: Cambridge University Press, 1971).

[10] *The Middle East and North Africa*, p. 65.

[11] Ibid., p. 66.

in July 1972. By the late 1950s it had become evident that the era of concessions in the D'Arcy tradition was over. The new concessions given by Abu Dhabi, Qatar and Dubai were limited in area, authority and profits. Also in the late 1950s new partnerships of governments and companies began to operate on new lands, thereby replacing the old system of concessions.

The most revolutionary change that has challenged the oil industry, as was shown above, came with the formation of OPEC. This organization has profoundly affected the oil industry in two areas: higher prices and participation of the governments with the companies in oil ownership, production and marketing. Partial ownership, ranging from 25 to 60 percent, by concessionary governments went into effect 1 January 1973, and the number of governments involved in partial ownership has continued to rise ever since.

A second development has been in the production increase of Middle East [12] oil and in the rise in the percentage of this production relative to total world production. In 1938 Middle Eastern oil production was 7.7 percent of total world production. By 1970 the figure had soared to 39.6 percent, to 40.4 percent in 1971, to 41.3 percent in 1972 [13] and to 49.1 percent in 1973.[14] American oil production in 1973 accounted for only 18.5 percent of the total world production; at the same time the United States was responsible for over 40 percent of total world consumption of energy. Table 7 vividly illustrates the dramatic rise in American oil imports over the last few years.

Related developments in the oil industry have been the sharp increases in the price of oil, the unprecedented revenues accumulated by the producing countries and the rising deficits in the trade balances of the consuming countries. Like all other consuming countries, the United States has felt the pressure of this gap between production and consumption. Between 1 January 1973 and 1 January 1974 Arab/Persian Gulf crude oil posted prices increased by 350 percent, from $2.59 per barrel to $11.65 per barrel,[15] and the OPEC governments' revenues (royalties plus taxes) for the same period rose by 358.1 percent or from $22.675 billion to $85.210 billion.[16] Throughout the

---

[12] For the purpose of this discussion, the term Middle East is used here to include the countries of the Fertile Crescent, the Arabian Peninsula, the Arab/Persian Gulf, Turkey and North Africa.

[13] *The Middle East and North Africa*, p. 75.

[14] Congressional Quarterly, *The Middle East*, p. 27.

[15] Ibid., p. 30.

[16] A slightly different picture is given when one considers the corrected oil revenues for the Arab/Persian Gulf countries alone, but the total picture of accumulated revenues remains substantially the same. See House Committee on Foreign Affairs, *New Perspectives on the Persian Gulf*, p. 155.

Table 7

U.S. TRADE IN CRUDE OIL

(thousands of barrels per day)

Year	Exports	Imports	Net Imports
1947	126	268	142
1948	110	353	244
1949	90	422	332
1950	96	488	392
1951	79	490	411
1952	74	575	501
1953	55	649	594
1954	38	658	619
1955	33	781	748
1956	79	937	858
1957	137	1,022	885
1958	11	953	942
1959	8	964	956
1960	8	1,019	1,011
1961	8	1,047	1,038
1962	5	1,126	1,121
1963	5	1,132	1,126
1964	3	1,203	1,200
1965	3	1,238	1,235
1966	5	1,225	1,219
1967	74	1,129	1,055
1968	5	1,293	1,288
1969	3	1,408	1,405
1970	14	1,323	1,310
1971	1	1,680	1,679
1972	*	2,222	2,222
1973 a	1	3,229	3,228

* Less than 500 barrels per day.

a Preliminary.

Source: Congressional Quarterly, *The Middle East: U.S. Policy, Israel, Oil and the Arabs* (Washington, D. C.: Congressional Quarterly Service, 1974), p. 26.

years, Saudi Arabia and Iran have received the lion's share of these revenues (see Table 8), which are expected to double by 1980. It is obvious that the United States, like other consuming countries, would like to retrieve some of its petrodollars either in the form of investment by oil-producing countries in the United States or by exporting American goods and services to these countries. What about the Arab gulf countries themselves?

It is obvious that oil is the one exportable commodity which they all have; they import most of their other products. More importantly, they are engaged in massive industrialization programs but lack trained manpower; their educational systems are embryonic; their revenues from agriculture (excluding Iraq) and other industries such as fishing are negligible as compared to their oil revenues. The total 1968 revenues for all nine amirates from vegetables, dates, fruits and alfalfa were under 7 million dollars.[17] The estimated total value for the same year from fishing and pearling was under 9 million dollars.[18]

Aside from the economics of oil and the complicated international financial transactions involved, the political aspects of the oil industry are the factors which have sparked the sensational events we have witnessed in the past two years. Oil has developed into a major determinant of policy in both the producing countries and the United States. Indeed, all of the goals and options discussed in the remainder of this chapter revolve around this issue.

Goals and Options: The Arab Gulf States

The heavy emphasis on oil in all Arab gulf states, the realization on the part of these states that oil is a finite natural resource and the availability of huge oil-generated revenues have created a need for long-range industrial planning whose function would be to expand the base of production and to prepare the economy for the post-oil era. Industrialization has been attempted through the building of energy-intensive industries for which oil or natural gas provides cheap fuel. These industries include the manufacture of aluminum, petrochemicals, cement, fertilizers, steel and liquid gas. But since the oil states have the same natural resource, the advantage for any one of them from this industrialization will be greatly reduced. Added to this, they lack the necessary human resources which would provide

---

[17] Frederick K. Lundy, "The Economic Prospects of the Persian Gulf Amirates" (unpublished manuscript, Washington, D. C., 1974), Table 14.
[18] Ibid., Table 15.

Table 8

ORGANIZATION OF PETROLEUM EXPORTING COUNTRIES' REVENUES [a] (1960–1980)
(in millions of dollars)

Country	1960	1965	1970	1971	1972	1973	1974	1975 [c]	1980 [c]
Saudi Arabia	$ 355	$ 655	$1,200	$ 2,101	$ 2,988	$ 4,915	$19,400	$22,850	$ 43,450
Kuwait	465	671	895	1,439	1,600	2,130	7,945	8,700	12,250
Abu Dhabi	[b]	33	233	418	538	1,035	4,800	6,550	14,750
Qatar	54	69	122	185	247	360	1,425	1,650	2,900
Iraq	266	375	521	840	802	1,465	5,900	7,550	16,750
Iran	285	522	1,093	1,934	2,423	3,885	14,930	17,100	30,700
Algeria	n.a.	n.a.	381	440	680	1,095	3,700	4,250	5,750
Libya	[b]	371	1,295	1,846	1,705	2,210	7,990	10,050	12,850
Nigeria	n.a.	n.a.	410	883	1,200	1,950	6,960	8,500	14,250
Indonesia	n.a.	n.a.	185	284	480	830	2,150	2,200	2,950
Venezuela	877	1,135	1,404	1,751	1,933	2,800	10,010	10,550	14,500
TOTAL	$2,303	$3,831	$7,742	$12,120	$14,515	$22,675	$85,210	$99,950	$171,100

a In November 1973 Ecuador became a member of OPEC and Gabon an associate member; they are not included in the above table.
b Libya and Abu Dhabi started production in 1961 and 1962, respectively.
c Medium estimates.

Source: Congressional Quarterly, *The Middle East: U.S. Policy, Israel, Oil and the Arabs* (Washington, D. C.: Congressional Quarterly Service, 1974), p. 34, with modifications.

a pool of technical and managerial skills for their industrialization programs.[19]

The future prospects for economic diversification in the gulf states will continue to be linked to oil, and opportunities for nonpetroleum-related industrial development seem to be very limited. The industries that the gulf states have already built, such as an aluminum smelter in Bahrain, a cement factory, flour mill and fertilizer factory in Qatar, a cement factory and a small aluminum manufactory in Dubai and a cement factory in Ra's al-Khayma, all seem to have the same marketing problems. Because of the limited nature of local markets, the gulf states must sell their products in foreign markets, where they are engaged in self-defeating competition against each other. It seems imperative that the Arab gulf states coordinate their industrial planning in order to complement each other and to avoid unnecessary duplication of efforts and facilities.[20]

In spite of the disadvantages mentioned above, economic diversification, primarily industrialization, remains a top priority national goal in all oil-producing countries. They all consider industrialization as the best way to provide for their peoples when the oil wells dry up. In Qatar, for example, the basic goal of industrial development is twofold: "To expand the productive base and to minimize the total reliance on only one source of income; and to build a balanced economy which would be able to face and overcome any potentially adverse developments in the oil sector—technological, international or political." [21]

Considering these goals, five options are available to the Arab gulf states for economic development:

(1) The Arab gulf countries should redouble their efforts toward economic cooperation on a regional level, something they have not yet fully accomplished for many political and traditional reasons. In a recent special United Nations study on economic prospects in the gulf, regional economic cooperation was emphatically recommended.[22]

---

[19] Ibid., p. iii.

[20] Muhammad T. Sadik and William P. Snavely, *Bahrain, Qatar and the United Arab Emirates: Colonial Past, Present Problems, and Future Prospects* (Lexington, Massachusetts: D. C. Heath and Company, 1972), pp. 61-62.

[21] Technical Center for Industrial Development, State of Qatar, *The Economic and Industrial Situation and Industrial Development Plans in the State of Qatar* (1974). An unpublished report presented to the Third Industrial Development Conference of the Arab States, held in Libya, 7-14 April 1974, pp. 1-21.

[22] United Nations Inter-Disciplinary Reconnaissance Mission, *Bahrain* (Beirut, Lebanon: United Nations Economic and Social Office, 1972). Similar studies were written on Qatar and Oman.

(2) A second option is to examine their future in terms of their human resources, which means they must intensify their efforts to provide a substantial cadre of professionally and technically trained nationals to staff their expanding economies.[23]

(3) Third, they must reexamine their educational systems in order to harmonize their developmental plans with their manpower planning.

(4) A fourth option is to intensify their efforts to devise a long-range developmental plan utilizing their presently available cheap energy, their available and potential manpower and the service of experts. According to Sadik and Snavely, these countries have often relied recently on the "friendly" advice of self-serving experts whose advice has often been "more costly than friendly."[24] The lack of trained manpower is considered the biggest problem in industrialization.[25]

(5) A fifth option would be to search for proper investment opportunities in which the Arab gulf states would be able to invest their surplus revenues, which their present economies have no capacity to absorb. At the same time, studies should be intensified concerning the expansion of these economies. It is this surplus, otherwise known as petrodollars, which the industrialized countries have been eyeing for possible investment. The oil-producing states have engaged in several forms of investment: banking in Europe, such as the Union de Banques Arabes et Francaises established in 1970; short-term investments through such institutions as the Kuwait Investment Company; traditional investment in European and American money markets (primarily Saudi reserves); and real estate investments, primarily Kuwaiti, in Europe and the United States.

Although "the day that the amirates will have to stand on what they have built, with no oil or gas to support it, is a long way off,"[26] they are all seriously searching for the best possible way to build viable post-oil economies. In the process it is probably natural and expected that some waste will occur and that mistakes will be made.

The more affluent and sophisticated of the Arab gulf states have expressed the desire to cooperate with the industrial countries of the West in the search for a better future. Both Shaikh Zaki Yamani, Saudi Arabia's minister of oil, and Yusif Shirawi, Bahrain's minister

[23] Ibid., pp. 14-15.

[24] Sadik and Snavely, *Bahrain, Qatar, and the United Arab Emirates*, p. 62.

[25] This problem was clearly stated at an OAPEC seminar on "Opportunities for Cooperation with the Arab World" held in London on 8 May 1974. See *Gulf Mirror* (Bahrain), 16 June 1974.

[26] Lundy, "The Economic Prospects of the Persian Gulf Amirates," p. iii.

of planning and engineering services, have publicly stated their willingness to enter into a new partnership with the West, to share the search for better ways in which Arab oil money could be utilized for the creation of a happier future for all mankind.[27] The call for cooperation and partnership with the West was best articulated by Yusif Shirawi. He said:

> Today, as we acknowledge our new role of strength, authority and power, we do so with a deep sense of humility. We feel that the world does not belong to the Arab world, but that the Arab world belongs to the world. We have a responsibility towards the world. We think that Western Europe has a responsibility towards us. If they want us to come into partnership with a capital "P," we have to wipe the slate clean and start with a new page, based not only on the normal values of fairness, justice and equality—that is not enough—but a deep sense of willingness to participate, willingness to share successes in human activity. Then we shall not feel that we are given only the second or the tourist class in the train of human progress but also the first class. We shall sit as equals.[28]

Goals and Options: The United States

Since American economic relations with the gulf center around oil, the United States's primary goal in the region may be succinctly defined as follows: to get as much oil as possible, as cheaply as possible, for as long as possible. As a counterview, and in the best tradition of free enterprise, the gulf states's obvious goal is to sell as much oil as possible, for as much as possible, for as long as possible. Diplomacy, the art of the possible, must harness these contradictory goals into a harmonious equilibrium. Although these two goals are by no means mutually exclusive, a considerable number of difficulties have hindered their fulfillment. The United States has discovered that it has had to pay high prices for oil; the gulf states have discovered that to keep prices high, they must cut back production. In addition, Saudi Arabia's minister of oil has recently stated that a ceiling must be placed on oil prices lest the world's economy be thrown into chaos.

In the light of these economic realities and until the United States becomes self-sufficient in energy, American policy makers

---

[27] *Gulf Mirror*, 9 June 1974 and 16 June 1974.
[28] *Gulf Mirror*, 16 June 1974.

must examine their options with regard to Arab oil anew. The first option calls for the establishment and perpetuation of friendly relations with the governments and peoples of the oil-producing countries, thereby creating an atmosphere conducive to concluding long-term commercial agreements on oil in terms of quantity and price. This atmosphere should help the United States pursue another option: the expansion of commercial relations whereby American exports to the gulf would be significantly increased. In 1972, the total of all American exports to all gulf countries, including Iran, was approximately 1.2 billion dollars, only 19 percent of the total world exports to the gulf. Half of the total American exports to the gulf in that year went to Iran, which means that American exports to the Arab gulf states, from Iraq to Oman, totaled a mere 600 million dollars. Obviously, this picture must be improved. (Table 9).

In order to encourage trade with the gulf, an imperative goal if the United States hopes to offset its balance of trade deficit caused by oil imports, the United States must intensify the efforts of the Department of Commerce as well as private companies to make American products known and attractive to gulf states. Representative teams of businessmen and Department of Commerce trade missions must frequent the gulf and exhibit their products. The trade missions in fiscal 1974 arranged by the Department of Commerce included educational equipment and materials, water resources development and communications equipment. The catalogue exhibits included industrial controls and hospital/medical equipment. The missions visited practically every major city in the gulf.[29] These laudable efforts must be made more frequently, and the Department of Commerce should help private American companies set up trade exhibits on a regular basis throughout the gulf displaying the entire range of American products, from test tubes to conveyor belts.

On another level, the United States should consider establishing economic ventures with gulf states on an equal basis. This type of partnership seems to be the only truly viable prospect for the future. An economic partnership, together with partnership in the political, social and cultural spheres, constitutes a basis for future healthy relations and ultimately the building of better societies in both the gulf and the United States.

---

[29] House Committee on Foreign Affairs, *New Perspectives on the Persian Gulf*, p. 162.

Table 9

1972 IMPORTS BY PERSIAN GULF COUNTRIES FROM THE UNITED STATES,
WESTERN EUROPE, AND JAPAN: VALUES (CIF) AND MARKET SHARES

(millions of dollars)

Importing Countries	World	Exporting Countries					
		United States		Western Europe [a]		Japan	
Saudi Arabia	$1,397	$ 346	25%	$ 445	34%	$265	19%
Kuwait	762	102	13	283	37	134	18
Iraq	843	26	3	313	37	35	4
United Arab Emirates	294	76	26	134	46	18	6
Oman	185	7	4	155	84	8	4
Bahrain	331	29	9	84	25	29	9
Qatar	102	15	15	67	65	—	—
Iran	2,675	617	23	1,368	51	358	13
TOTAL	$6,589	$1,217	19%	$2,848	44%	$846	13%

[a] United Kingdom and "Industrialized Europe" (Austria, Belgium, Denmark, France, West Germany, Italy, Netherlands, Norway, Sweden, Switzerland).

Source: New Perspectives on the Persian Gulf, 93d Congress, 1st session (Washington, D. C.: U.S. Government Printing Office, 1973), p. 155.

4

THE UNITED STATES AND
THE ARAB/PERSIAN GULF:
A FRAMEWORK FOR PARTNERSHIP

An Overview

The key element of any future American policy in the gulf should be partnership. Broadly defined, the partnership model would be a functional system of bilateral and regional relationships between the United States and the Arab countries of the gulf that would generally identify American long-range interests and goals in that region and would hopefully encourage gulf governments to view American interest in regional peace and stability as complementary to their own goals and aspirations. This system of relationships would be solidly based on the twin principles, which must be frequently reiterated to gulf governments, that an American presence would not preempt the presence, posture and prominence of local governments and that the United States's real concern for prosperity, peace and security would not mean that Washington would dictate policy— covertly or overtly—to gulf governments. American policy makers should emphasize to these governments that American concern for peace and security is a universal principle which transcends any one region. Armed with a belief in the universality of this principle, the United States can forge this new system of partnership, utilizing a clear concept and a well-defined method of achieving the desired structure.

Although the proposed partnership is a sharp departure from general American policy in the gulf in recent years, it does offer a combination of morality and national interest [1] which should not be

---

[1] A mixture of morality and national interest in American foreign policy was eloquently advocated in Robert J. Pranger, *American Policy for Peace in the Middle East, 1969-1971* (Washington, D. C.: American Enterprise Institute for Public Policy Research, 1971), p. 5. "The United States needs peace," wrote Pranger, "to convince itself that its international commitments over the past years have not been in vain: that the good of mankind has been served by extensive United States activities in the world and that its own domestic society has benefited."

rejected outright on the grounds of idealism or of novelty. Partnership should be presented to policy makers as a promoter of a better world and a more viable America. American commitment to peace (a moral goal) and its quest for markets (a national interest goal) are ultimately the two sides of the same coin. It is heartening to hear leaders throughout the Arab gulf, as this author has heard in the last two years, openly state that the United States is the only country that is traditionally equipped to bring about peace and prosperity in the world.

The proposed partnership policy must be tried, not as a matter of academic curiosity but as an urgently needed substitute for our present relations. This is not just a call for a new general policy. Rather, partnership is a prescription for a specific kind of policy. In this context, the proposed partnership emerges as the only viable, functional, long-range option for the United States in the Arab/Persian Gulf in the coming decade. For the new partnership to endure, it must be creative, multidimensional, mutually beneficial, and open, that is, subject to scrutiny. The absence of one or more of these elements will contribute to trouble, and a troubled partnership is a sure formula for future conflict.

Creative Partnership

In order to translate the rhetoric of partnership into policy, United States decision makers must first recognize the post-October War realities of the Middle East—on both sides of the Arabian Peninsula.[2] The psychological rejuvenation of the Arab psyche brought about by the October War cannot be overemphasized. For the first time, Arab oil producers effectively used oil as a weapon for political purposes. The devastating impact of the selective oil sanctions imposed during and since the October War was mainly due to the logical reasoning and thorough planning used in the boycott.

It is this new-found power of rational planning that has lifted the Arab psyche to new heights. As one official in a gulf country told this author, the era of the organization man has finally dawned in the Arab world! Oil-producing countries such as Saudi Arabia and other gulf states have shown an ability to make and implement policy concerning oil, regionally and internationally, that has surprised the most sophisticated policy practitioners in the Western world. No

---

[2] At the risk of being trite, one can safely state that whatever the final military outcome, the October War was a watershed in the psychological makeup and morale of all Arab people.

longer can the foreign-based oil companies or the industrial consuming countries dictate policies to Arabia's rulers or governments, as was the case up until the late sixties. Times have simply changed, and American policy makers must adjust their concepts to the new realities. Seen in this context, an American-Arab creative partnership in the gulf can definitely develop.

The need for a creative partnership can be seen in another area as well. Although technically Arab gulf countries are still developing, the enormous oil revenues which they have amassed have given them two advantages rarely enjoyed by other developing countries: the power to purchase the most sophisticated technology and scientific expertise and the independence to shop around for this technology. They no longer turn automatically to the United Kingdom or to the United States for the advanced products of modern technology. Japan, China and even India, three major non-Western countries, will be able to offer very vigorous competition to Western technology within the coming half decade. Any American-Arabian gulf partnership must take this trade competition into consideration, especially when one weighs the number of foreign businessmen swarming into the gulf, from Kuwait in the north to Oman in the south.

A third reality that American policy makers charged with building the new partnership in the gulf must consider is the intense, unrelenting competition among Western (that is, American, British, French, German, and Dutch) businessmen themselves in the gulf. Political alliances and understandings among Western democracies are inoperative in the economic world. The brutal competition for contracts, tenders and projects among Western industrial concerns in the gulf is but another manifestation of economic nationalism, which the present nation-state system unfortunately seems to nurture. American policy makers will do well to recognize this phenomenon.

At least two positions have developed within the United States government on this question. The first position, that of traditional laissez-faire economics, basically supports free competition and maintains that the only edge American firms hope to gain over others in the gulf, and indeed elsewhere, is in the quality of goods and services rendered. Advocates of this position have relied on the internationally recognized high standards of American technology and the respected quality of American products to promote American business interests abroad. The second position, however, has called for more direct government involvement in this matter. The United States government, advocates of this position maintain, must either aid American companies overseas in negotiating collectively with the countries involved, as the major oil companies were allowed to do in the fifties and sixties in Iran and elsewhere, or in initiating contacts with some European governments for reaching certain understandings on some sort of a unified Western economic policy in the gulf. Whatever course of action is finally adopted, the issue of economic nationalism will remain for the foreseeable future, and American economic interests will have to be worked out in this context.

In addition to political and economic creativity, a creative partnership must also be able to operate outside the bounds of any particular status quo at any given time. Such a partnership should not be dependent on any specific regime or system of government for its survival. In other words, a partnership system of relationships must be able to transcend personalities. Such a recommendation may seem at first glance to be extremely difficult, if not actually impossible, to implement, especially since in the new gulf countries rulers, not governments, personally run the affairs of state. Yet at the same time American policy makers must also realize that, in spite of its advantages, personal rule, as compared to institutional government, has at least one major flaw: because it is unpredictable, its survival is always in question. A creative partnership must be able to strike a balance between the religious, tribal and cultural sources of authority of a specific rule in the gulf and the exercise of force and power upon which such a rule is based.

To illustrate, the Islamic principle of *shura* (consultation) remains a cornerstone of rule in every Arab gulf state, although the degree of adherence to this principle varies from one state to the next. Direct contact between the ruler and his people is another tribal principle that gulf rulers try to maintain even today. Most rulers hold a daily *majlis* (gathering) which may be attended by any citizen, and the citizen thereby brings his problem directly and openly to the ruler.

It must be remembered that *shura* is not synonymous with participatory democracy nor is it synonymous with any concept of modern democracy as it is known and practiced in the West. *Shura* means that the ruler receives the views of the elders in the community, formally or informally, but it does not mean that he is obligated to heed these views. The *shura* tradition must be viewed in its tribal/Islamic context, without the embellishments of Western academe.

In combination with these two religious/tribal principles of *shura* and *majlis*, Arab gulf countries are in the process of establishing a modern public administration, a functioning governmental machinery and a complex infrastructure. Gulf rulers have shown a serious desire to translate the sources of force and power, both physical and cultural, upon which their personal rule is based into a system of authority for governing. A creative partnership must comprehend the very delicate process of this transformation from classical tribalism into modern statehood.

A creative partnership must avoid being rigid in either structure or purpose. It must have a built-in flexibility which could absorb any political or economic shocks along the way. During the formative years of nation building, which the Arab littoral of the gulf is presently experiencing, any disturbance of even a minor nature may potentially assume the magnitude of a crisis. Lack of experience in the affairs of state in the new countries and the absence of institutional government invariably promote an atmosphere in which small disputes within governmental departments or even among different governments threaten to blow up into full-fledged crises. Whatever shocks develop, a creative partnership should be able to absorb their waves.

A creative partnership must also carry within it the seeds of regeneration and rejuvenation. A relationship based on partnership must be able to grow; it must be part of a process of becoming. Such a partnership must be equipped from within to offer new alternatives. The ability to grow is a sign of health, and only a healthy partnership endures. Moreover, because of its ability to rejuvenate, the partnership itself, and not the individual partners, would always remain the focus of the relationship. Once the individual partners feel that they can go it alone, the partnership is superfluous; in this event, American long-range interests in the gulf, the object of this partnership, would be placed in an untenable position. To avoid this end, American policy makers in charge of this partnership must have the courage to experiment with new forms of partnerships and relationships within the broad framework of American relations with the gulf. The simple fact of signing an agreement specifying a certain relationship, no matter how beneficial to the United States at the time it is concluded, must not halt the search for feasible alternatives.

Finally, a creative partnership must be both descriptive and prescriptive. Although this model of relationships has been created with present realities in mind, both within gulf societies and within the United States, it is also designed to serve a higher goal than national interest. Through partnership it is hoped that a better world would be created and a more promising future for the American people and the peoples of the gulf region could be realized. Moral ends and national interest can be reconciled into a new synthesis of human understandings. A partnership model may represent our view of prosperity and security based on present assessments, yet it must also be a prescription for a preferred world in which the United States national interest, based on rationality, common sense and courage, may live in peace and harmony with the national interests of other states in the region.

A Multidimensional Partnership

Partnership between the United States and the Arab gulf states must be multidimensional, functioning simultaneously on at least two levels: political and economic. Through a multidimensional approach, a proposed policy of partnership could also become a program of action. Such an all-encompassing partnership would enable the United States to play a positive, and hopefully welcome, role in helping the new states of the gulf transform their tribal societies into modern states. Rulers and ruling families of these political communities know very well that the tribal structure which has supported their societies in the past is rapidly breaking down. A new order of plenty is setting in; however, the birth of the new order, unlike the experience of Western societies since the industrial revolution, has not been the result of a well-planned pregnancy. The advent of plenty and the phenomenon of affluence have been abrupt, massive and socially disturbing changes. Unlike the experience of most developing countries, the problems of development present in the gulf are not a result of want and poverty. The sociocultural disturbances of affluence are a new phenomenon, one which is widely felt but barely understood.

If the United States hopes to embark on a partnership with the new countries of the gulf, American policy planners must be fully cognizant of this process of societal transformation. A warning at this juncture: American policy makers must be extremely careful lest their attitude concerning the future course of development in the gulf be viewed by gulf leaders as paternalistic. The recommended partnership is designed to discourage that form of relationship.

On the political level, American-Arab partnership in the gulf must address itself to at least four fundamental issues: (1) the making of the new states, (2) political reform and the entire process of evolutionary political development, (3) tribal sources of legitimacy and popular demands for participation, and (4) the establishment of

74

modern government machinery. The United States cannot expect to enter into long-range relations with individual gulf countries without full awareness of the structures of the states involved and the internal political dynamics of the regimes.

Knowledge of local conditions would include the ruling family in each of these states, the history and ascendancy to power of each ruling family, the hereditary distribution of power within the family itself and the political relationship among the various ruling families in the region. In addition, the type of regime and the real sources of power within the regime must be well understood. Does a certain ruler, for example, base his authority on his charismatic leadership, on tribal customs, on the exercise of brute force or on a quasi-popular acceptance of his regime? In such a case legitimacy becomes a real factor that must be contended with.

American policy makers in charge of this country's future in the gulf must also be cognizant of the actual management of political affairs within the individual states. Who exercises authority? Who benefits from the system? Who are the dissatisfied and the dis-inherited? What is the nature of the opposition to the regime? Has it been co-opted and how? These questions must be asked if one reasonably expects to engage in any long-term relationship with a particular regime in any one of the Arab gulf countries.

The demographic nature of these countries must also be probed; the level of education, the structure of the educated elites, the labor force and the ethnic background of the working classes are all obvious points of analysis. Since generalized answers usually fail to truly reflect the realities of each society, a more detailed knowledge of the individual societies must be obtained. To illustrate, the labor tradition and the level of education which exist in Bahrain are unparalleled in the lower gulf; therefore such an issue as unionization, a paramount political topic in Bahrain for decades, is somewhat alien to other gulf countries. Also unknown in gulf countries other than Bahrain is the plight of the unemployed intelligentsia. Another example would be the variations in population levels: whereas most of the Arab gulf states are underpopulated, Bahrain suffers from serious over-population.[3]

In addition to understanding the new political formations taking shape in the Arab littoral states, an Arab-American partnership in

---

[3] See *Population and the Future of Bahrain*, a 1973 study prepared by William P. McGreevey of the International Program for Population Analysis (Smithsonian Institution) and Steven W. Sinding of the Agency for International Development (U.S. Department of State).

the region must consider the broader question of political reform. Since political stability is a prerequisite for any lasting relationship, American policy makers must realize that political reform from within these regimes is ultimately the only enduring guarantor of stability. The use of force to fight a rebellion in Dhufar or to liquidate a leftist movement in Bahrain might be an effective short-term measure, but it is ineffective and counterproductive in the long run. A multidimensional partnership would eventually require the United States to actively engage in a political dialogue with gulf elites concerning the prospects for political stability and the nature of political reform in those societies. A case can be made, philosophically and practically, that internal reform and political evolution from within are the only sure ways to thwart revolution.

The transformation from classical tribalism into the modern state essentially involves a dilution of previously unquestioned autocratic tribal rule. This transformation also brings about a change in the nature of the people of the new political community: from ruled into governed, from subjects into citizens. The Sabah ruling family of Kuwait and the Khalifa ruling family of Bahrain, much to their credit, have been able to comprehend this transformation and to adjust to it.

Another important point in a multidimensional partnership is the changing nature of tribal legitimacy in the face of certain local demands for popular participation in government. Attempts along these lines have been initiated in most gulf countries. Kuwait promulgated a constitution and established a parliament in 1961, Bahrain followed suit in 1973, and Qatar established an Advisory Council (*Majlis al-Shura*) in 1972. Abu Dhabi also established an Advisory Council in 1971. The rest of the amirates still rely primarily on personal rule. The Kuwaiti and Bahraini constitutional experiments are the pacesetters for a slow and gradual sharing of authority within the political structures of the gulf. Those ruling families who possess the ability to adjust to change will survive; the others will fall. Partnership can play a positive role in the widening of the popular base of government in these societies.

On the economic level, Arab-American partnership can play a very effective role in the gulf. The United States can significantly contribute to the new economic structures of gulf societies—contributions which will benefit all parties of the partnership. The United States can provide assistance, on a reimbursable basis, in managerial methods, banking and investment, development planning and statistical and manpower expertise. Of course economic partnership between the United States and the countries of the gulf would naturally involve long-term trade agreements on oil, gas, import-export, and general trade.

Although committed to partnership, the United States would not be expected to dictate the direction or type of economic development which these countries should follow nor should the United States attempt to influence the choice which those governments make in selecting a particular economic ideology. The American style of private enterprise cannot be offered as a model of economic development nor would it necessarily work in those societies should the regimes decide to emulate it. This is not to say that American policy makers should be oblivious to economic planning in the region or that the absence of American-tailored private enterprise would automatically pave the way for Marxist socialism.

The economic ideology that seems to be developing in the gulf may best be described as *étatisme*. The state owns most of the wealth, in oil as well as in other major industries, such as flour mills, cement factories, fertilizers, aluminum smelters, steel mills and petrochemicals. Significantly, over 80 percent of the labor force in every gulf country is employed in the public sector, and in each of these countries the government bureaucracy is usually the largest employer. It is worth noting that teachers, like other employees of the ministries of education, are part of the civil service. Also included in the public sector are the various governments' large share in banking, import-export and the import and marketing of such basic foodstuffs as flour, sugar, rice and meat. In most gulf countries, the government also plays a significant role in the local chamber of commerce. Every major economic project is government planned, approved, controlled and at least partially financed.

Philosophically, *étatisme* in the Arab gulf states may be viewed as a logical development of the Islamic concept of the state, especially as it applies to the responsibility of the ruler toward his people. On a practical level, *étatisme* developed naturally from the fact that in pre-oil tribal societies, the ruler and his family traditionally owned most of the sources of wealth in each society—real estate, the pearl trade, and general commerce. The discovery of oil did not alter the authority of these rulers. They granted concessions, received royalties and began to amass great wealth. In each of these societies, four or five families rivaled the ruling family in prominence, wealth, and influence, but the majority of the population remained dependent on the state for economic well-being. *Etatisme* was the logical result of these conditions.

Several gulf rulers have recently expressed the desire to expand the base of wealth in their countries, and this could coincide well with the proposed model of partnership. The United States could play a crucial and positive role in this expansion of the economic base in these societies. The two most immediate areas requiring attention are the building of an economic infrastructure and manpower planning. This is where American technical expertise can be put to good use, especially since most gulf governments have recognized the need in these two areas and have approached outside governments, including the United States, for expert advice. American technical experts have already been assigned to certain gulf countries through the United Nations's specialized agencies, private foundations and corporations.[4] All of these states have initiated manpower studies to determine present and future manpower needs for their industrialization, and the United States, within a partnership framework, should be able to contribute to these studies by providing experts in statistics, manpower, labor and employment, population, vocational training, and management and administration. The nationalization of labor in several of these countries has become a serious national goal, and the United States has the resources to contribute to the attainment of this goal.

The United States can also contribute to the building of an economic infrastructure in these countries as well. Public transportation is a good example of this type of contribution. It was an American expert who in 1972 established a relatively functional public transportation system in Bahrain. Cooperation in the technical field can also be expected to function reasonably well, since the American approach to assistance is usually not elitist, colonial or paternalistic. Governments in these states have themselves recognized the need for technical assistance, and they have already employed a good number of consultants in this area. All of these states have also established manpower councils, industrial development centers and vocational training departments. Through partnership American technology and technical expertise could contribute significantly to the betterment of these societies, and their governments would gladly pay for these services.

Mutually Beneficial Partnership

For any long-range partnership between the United States and the Arab gulf states to endure, it must be designed to benefit all parties.

---

[4] As an illustration, there was an ILO expert in Qatar (1974), a TWA transportation expert in Bahrain (1972), and a Ford manpower expert in Bahrain (1973).

American economic and strategic interests can best be served only when local governments are convinced that their relationship with the United States does not benefit America at their expense. The United States attitude toward sharing the gains from this relationship should be one of let-us-benefit-together. Such mutual benefits would occur in three main areas: economic, strategic, and cultural.

American-Arab partnership can bring economic advantages to both sides. Any long-term trade agreements could open up new markets for American products while affording gulf governments and private firms reasonably secure investment opportunities in the United States. The sale of American machinery and appliances should always offer new possibilities for training local young men in American training centers. Agreements for the purchase of oil might be accompanied by further agreements in local industrialization programs.

In sum, American-Arab economic agreements in the gulf would assure the United States of at least two valuable benefits: the guaranteed flow of oil and a partial return of oil dollars to the United States. Gulf countries would also benefit in at least two areas. They would align themselves with the world's most advanced and most stable economy, and in their industrialization endeavor they would draw on the most sophisticated technology and industrial and scientific knowledge available to any nation. This posited end does not mean that the road to partnership is easy. Competition by Japanese and European firms and some politically inspired residual negative attitudes within certain gulf countries are two factors that will slow the growth of economic partnership in the gulf. Nevertheless, the genuine respect sensed in the region for American technology is a strong persuasive factor in the equation of cooperation.

Mutual advantages accruing from partnership are also evident in the area of military strategy. At the risk of being trite, one must again emphasize the strategic importance of the Arab/Persian Gulf to Western security. The United States has obviously recognized this fact, and for over a generation the American navy has been at least symbolically present in gulf waters. As a source of political stability, the United States presence in the gulf would serve the interests of all parties. Political stability would minimize the level of tension, which in turn would decrease the likelihood of political confrontation. Also, the containment of radicalism would make it possible for the region's governments to mature politically and hopefully to govern ultimately in the spirit of reason and compromise. Given this turn of events, American interests might reasonably expect to endure for a considerable length of time. Political stability and economic prosperity

would also, as a corollary benefit, make it difficult for political revolutionism, supported by either the Soviet Union or China, to succeed
in these societies. Simultaneously, the United States should also
encourage gulf governments to set in motion a guided, continuing
process of political reform.

The Jufair agreement, as was mentioned earlier, once it is renego-
tiated might well become a model of the type of cooperation which
benefits both sides. A symbolic American navy presence in the gulf
in the form of frequent friendly visits to the shores of the Arab littoral
states would indicate to these governments America's interest in
peace and friendship, and American military interests would be well
served by having this foothold in the Arab/Persian Gulf. The United
States, however, must be willing to pay a reasonable price, primarily
in technical assistance, for the use of homeporting facilities, be it in
Bahrain or in any other gulf country. Such a price would obviously
have to be commensurate with the need for such facilities, and
American policy makers should also be prepared to grant the host
country the right to freely decide whether the price it is getting for
the homeporting facilities is worth the risk of potential radical
attacks on this form of cooperation and whether it is sufficient induce-
ment for the leaders of that country to become entangled in superpower politics. To repeat, the Jufair agreement is a lesson worth
learning.

On the cultural level, partnership could offer enticing benefits
to all parties. Education and educational-cultural exchanges of students, teachers and experts would be of interest to the United States
and would be a substantial benefit to the countries of the gulf.
American methods in education could play a positive role in modern-
izing the educational systems of all the gulf countries. Although only
Kuwait and Saudi Arabia have national universities, other countries,
such as Bahrain, Qatar and the United Arab Emirates, have already
established teacher-training colleges. Qatar hopes that its College
of Education will act as a nucleus for a future national university.
Several education officials in these countries have already turned to
the American government and American private institutions for
advice on curricular development, and the expansion of such cooperation would be economically advantageous to the United States, especially in the sale of educational equipment such as laboratory
apparatus and audio-visual equipment.

In addition, American institutions of higher learning, faced with
a shrinking student population in America, could hope to attract
many potential students from the gulf. Cultural exchanges could also

be established and maintained on the professorial level, as well as on a high administrative level. The prejudices of previous years would hopefully dissipate once the Islamic Arab culture of the gulf and the American culture find common ground for deeper understanding of each other. On a higher level, extensive contacts between these two cultures would definitely tend to bring them together instead of keeping them apart.

Open Partnership

In the final analysis, American-Arab cooperation in the gulf and elsewhere must be a product of open communication and the clear understanding of the interests, short term and long term, of all the countries involved. Whatever treaties, agreements and understandings are concluded between the United States and the countries of this region, they must be subject to the scrutiny of the American Congress and people and the peoples of the region. An open approach to international agreements does not necessarily undermine the security of the states involved, as some staunch advocates of the nation-state system would have it. When agreements are concluded with the knowledge of the peoples of the concerned governments, those agreements have a reasonable chance of survival.

To establish an open relationship with the countries of the gulf, the American approach must have courage and understanding. American policy makers must have the moral courage to explain American economic, commercial, strategic and human interests to gulf governments in clear and precise terms. All states constantly attempt to improve their position in international politics and to optimize the policy options available to them. States are constantly searching for new markets and for economic progress, and the Arab gulf countries need world markets for their oil and other industrial products. Therefore it would not surprise them to hear that the United States, too, searches for new markets for its products.

American policy makers must also have the courage to assure gulf leaders that partnership does not preclude the existence of differences of opinion on certain political issues. Cooperation is not necessarily synonymous with conformity. Differences of opinion are in fact the mark of a healthy relationship. Finally, the United States must have the courage to explain that American interests, economic or strategic, transcend the gulf region. Being a superpower, the United States concerns for peace, security, and prosperity are worldwide.

At the same time, the United States must show a genuine understanding of the problems of the region and must be demonstrably aware of the as yet unresolved political questions which concern the governments and peoples of the region. The newly independent countries of the gulf are presently passing through a very delicate stage of national development; being in the limelight of international politics has not been easy for them. They are embryonic political communities, and they are experimenting with unfamiliar methods of government. These governments are uneasy about this experimentation, and they consequently value their privacy highly. American policy makers should be aware of the process of transformation which these societies are undergoing, and they must be sensitive to the pains of this transformation.

Awareness of societal transformation in these countries demands fundamental knowledge of the basic components of Arab civilization: religion, history, language, and culture. In a sense, this is a call for a clearly defined approach to diplomacy based on scholarship. With these guidelines in mind, a new relationship with the Arab/Persian Gulf countries is possible, and American long-range interests can be well served within the framework of this proposed partnership.